ESSEN'

GW00514841

CHINA

★ Best places to see 34–55

■ Featured sight

Written by Graham Bond and Paul Mooney

© Automobile Association Developments Limited 2008
First published 2008

ISBN: 978-0-7495-5353-1

Published by AA Publishing, a trading name of Automobile Association Developments
Limited, whose registered office is Fanum House, Basing View, Basingstoke,
Hampshire RG21 4EA.
Registered number 1878835.

A CIP catalogue record for this book is available from the British Library

Colour separation: MRM Graphics Ltd
Printed and bound in Italy by Printer Trento S.r.l.

A03164
Maps in this title produced from mapping © MAIRDUMONT / Falk Verlag 2007
Additional data from Mountain High Maps® Copyright © 1993 Digital Wisdom, Inc
Transport map © Communicarta Ltd, UK

About this book

Symbols are used to denote the following categories:

✚ map reference to maps on cover

✉ address or location

☎ telephone number

🕐 opening times

✋ admission charge

🍴 restaurant or café on premises or nearby

Ⓜ nearest underground train station

🚍 nearest bus/tram route

🚊 nearest overground train station

⛴ nearest ferry stop

✈ nearest airport

❓ other practical information

ℹ tourist information office

► indicates the page where you will find a fuller description

---

This book is divided into five sections:

The essence of China pages 6–19
Introduction; Features; Food and drink; Short break

Planning pages 20–33
Before you go; Getting there; Getting around; Being there

Best places to see pages 34–55
The unmissable highlights of any visit to China

Best things to do pages 56–69
Great places to have lunch; places to take the children; stunning views and more

Exploring pages 70–185
The best places to visit in China, organized by area

Maps All map references are to the maps on the covers. For example, Yangshuo has the reference ✚ 2K – indicating the grid square in which it is to be found

Admission prices
Inexpensive (under 30RMB)
Moderate (30–100RMB)
Expensive (over 100RMB)

Hotel prices Prices are per room and per night excluding breakfast:
$ inexpensive (under 500RMB);
$$ moderate (500–1500RMB);
$$$ expensive to luxury (over 1500RMB)

Restaurant prices Average prices for a meal for two excluding drinks:
$ inexpensive (under 100RMB);
$$ moderate (100–250RMB);
$$$ expensive (over 250RMB)

Contents

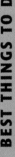

BEST THINGS TO DO

EXPLORING...

The essence of...

Few countries have developed as rapidly as China over the past two decades. Deng Xiaoping launched economic reforms in 1979, improving the lives of the Chinese in both urban and rural areas. Despite these changes, the essence of the country still lies in its long history and rich heritage. Wherever you go, history is there in the background, from the historical dramas on the TV, through to the cartoons and comics enjoyed by school children. More concrete traces can be found in every city and village: ancient wooden pagodas, magnificent imperial palaces and tombs, classic gardens, medieval city walls and beautiful scenery.

THE ESSENCE OF CHINA

features

A story is often told about Arthur Waley (1889–1966), the eminent translator who introduced Chinese literature to Western readers for the first time in the early 1900s. Waley had never been to China, but decided he would sail there to see the land he had been so intimately involved with. According to the story, the boat arrives in the harbour, but Waley has second thoughts. He realises the country will bear no resemblance to the China of his translations and decides not to disembark. He sails back to England a few days later having never set foot on Chinese soil, but with his idyllic image of China still intact.

Many visitors to China may share Waley's concern. The China they experience will bear little resemblance to the one seen in movies or read about in books. China is a country of sharp contrasts. Walk around an isolated village and you'll see satellite dishes poking from crumbling tiled roofs. Yet nearby farmers manually irrigate fields in much the same way as their grandfathers did.

China continues to grapple with the problem of how to preserve its ancient past, while also providing its people with the modernity and comforts they crave.

GEOGRAPHY

● China covers an area of 9.6 million sq km (3.7 million sq miles). The country is bordered by Russia and Mongolia to the north, North Korea to the east, Vietnam, Laos, Myanmar, India, Bhutan and Nepal to the south, and Pakistan, Afghanistan, Tajikistan, Kyrgyzstan and Kazakhstan to the west.
● China is divided into 22 provinces,

five autonomous regions and four independent municipalities. Hong Kong, a British colony since 1841, was returned to China in 1997, and Macau, settled by the Portuguese in 1557, was made a part of China again in 1999.

CLIMATE
● Because of the size of the country, there are great variations in climate and temperatures, from Siberian conditions during the winter in the far north to tropical humid weather in the south, and desert conditions in the northwest. The best times to visit are spring (April–May) and autumn (October–November).
● Travellers are advised to wear layers of clothing in the winter and light clothing in the heat.

PEOPLE
● China has a population of 1.3 billion people. Some 92 per cent are Han people, or ethnic Chinese, with 8 per cent belonging to one of 55 different ethnic/linguistic groups.
● Most Chinese speak Putonghua (Mandarin), the official national language based on the Beijing dialect. Chinese ideographic writing is the same everywhere.

CHINESE NAMES
● Chinese surnames traditionally precede the given name and this is the system used in this book. It is customary to address people by their surnames followed by Xiansheng (Mr), or Xiaojie (Ms). For younger people, including tour guides, it is common to precede the surname with the familiar title 'Xiao', or little, ie Xiao Wang.

THE ESSENCE OF CHINA

food & drink

China has a wide variety of regional cuisines, with each province having its own specialty. The following are the more popular cuisines that can be found around the country.

BEIJING

Mild, but hearty. Wheat, rather than rice is the staple and dumplings, breads and noodles feature prominently. The most famous dish is Peking duck. The meat and crisp skin of the duck and sliced spring onions or cucumbers are wrapped in thin crêpes of slightly griddled, unleavened dough dabbed with sweet soybean paste. Soup made from the duck bones is also delicious.

SICHUAN

Spicy and richly flavoured, this cuisine makes liberal use of hot peppers. Popular specialties include *gongbao chicken* (diced, boneless chicken sautéed with chillies), aubergine with garlic and *mapo tofu* (diced bean curd sautéed with ground pork, garlic, spring onions, ginger and lots of chilli peppers). Instead of rice, try *yinzi juan,* a delicious roll steamed or deep-fried.

HUNAN

The Hunanese are also known for their liberal use of chilli peppers. The home of the late Chairman Mao Zedong, Hunan has many restaurants which specialize in the favourites of the former leader.

JIANGZHE

The highlight of this cuisine (from Jiangsu and Zhejiang, two provinces located on the east coast), is seafood. This style is also known as Shanghai-style cooking.

CANTONESE

Cooking from Guangdong Province in southern China is lighter and less sweet compared to other cuisines. The Cantonese are famous for eating just about every type of animal. According to one popular saying, they will eat 'everything with legs except a table, everything with wings except airplanes, and everything under the sea except submarines'. Cantonese food is perhaps most famous for the breakfast and lunchtime snacks known as dim sum, or *dian xin* in Mandarin. Waitresses wheel carts loaded with steam baskets through the restaurant and diners select what they want from the parade of dumplings, pastries and roasted and steamed treats.

VEGETARIAN

Called *su cai,* vegetarian dishes have long been a part of Chinese cuisine and contrary to popular opinion, are anything but bland. This cuisine is served at Buddhist temples and restaurants around the country.

ETIQUETTE

Chinese dishes are ordered communally, with guests helping themselves from the collection placed in the centre of the table. It is good manners to take from each dish what can be eaten immediately; do not accumulate a great pile of food on your side plate or in your rice bowl. In many restaurants there is no side plate, and so you are expected to use the rice bowl as the resting place for food taken

from the communal dishes. If there is a serving spoon or chopsticks, use them to select your chosen dish; otherwise it's acceptable to use your chopsticks to take food directly from the communal plate. Watch your Chinese friends or neighbouring diners closely and act accordingly. It may be acceptable to sip soup directly from your soup bowl if others are doing so.

ALCOHOLIC DRINKS
Virtually all restaurants in China – unless they are Muslim – serve alcohol in the form of beer or rice wine. Imported spirits and wines are usually only available at more fashionable restaurants and bars.

BEVERAGES
While tea is the standard beverage served at meals, restaurants also serve a wide variety of soft drinks, mineral waters, juices, and alcoholic

beverages, including an increasingly wide variety of wines in better establishments. Chinese are serious beer drinkers, and just about every town has at least one brewery, so when travelling try the local brews. A Chinese favourite is baijiu, a grain-based, potent beverage.

DRINKING ETIQUETTE

When dining in a more formal setting, guests usually do not drink individually. It is considered polite to wait for the host or another guest to toast you before drinking from your glass. You may also like to offer a toast to others sitting at the table. Make eye contact with your intended target and raise your glass with two hands, tipping it slightly in his or her direction. After taking a drink, hold out the glass in the direction of the person to show how much you've consumed. It's common for Chinese friends to try to get you to drink a lot, and you will often hear the toast *ganbei*, or 'bottoms up'. If you don't like to finish your drink in a single gulp, you can just say *suiyi*, or 'how you wish', which means either party can drink as much as the person likes.

CHOPSTICKS

It's a good idea to learn how to use a pair of chopsticks in China, as their use is so widespread. Hold the chopsticks about two-thirds from the bottom, leaning them against the web between your thumb and index finger. Use the index and middle fingers as a fulcrum to manoeuvre the two sticks. Do not stand your chopsticks into your bowl of rice – which resembles incense placed in a bowl in a funeral service – but place them on the chopstick holder, or across your bowl. Also remember not to lay them down pointing in the direction of other guests, which is considered rude.

short break

If you only have a short time in which to visit China and want to get under the skin of the country and of Chinese culture, here are some essentials:

● **Wander around a park** early in the morning for a look at how Chinese start their day. You'll see people doing ballroom and disco dancing, callisthenics and martial arts.

● **Go fly a kite:** kite flying is a favourite pastime among youngsters and senior citizens and takes place in large open spaces, such as Tiananmen Square (► 84–85) in Beijing.

● **Visit a karaoke parlour:** while many Westerners are put off by the idea of performing at a karaoke, it's a national pastime for the Chinese. A good voice is not required.

● **Enjoy Peking duck** at one of Beijing's numerous duck outlets. Spread the thin pancake with plum sauce, layer with spring onion or cucumber, and stuff with crispy pieces of skin and meat.

● **Ride a bike:** with Chinese city streets becoming increasingly clogged with private cars, the bicycle remains the most stress-free means of sightseeing. Be warned, drivers are not known for their consideration for cyclists.

● **Hop on a pedicab:** take a tour of the back streets on a pedal-powered carriage, stopping wherever something catches your interest.

● **See an opera:** different regions boast their own operatic styles, but all feature melodramatic plots, highly stylized acting and magnificent costumes.

● **Take the train:** share a bag of sunflower seeds and a cup of cha with the locals during a train ride to one of your destinations. Soft-sleeper berths accommodate four people in a closed room, while hard-sleeper berths have six beds in an open cubicle.

● **Visit a produce market:** wander around during the early morning or just after work as Chinese housewives choose fresh ingredients for the family meal.

● **Visit a tea house:** finish off the day with a visit to a traditional tea house, where tea is slowly brewed in tiny pots.

Planning

Before you go

WHEN TO GO

JAN	FEB	MAR	APR	MAY	JUN	JUL	AUG	SEP	OCT	NOV	DEC
1°C	4°C	11°C	21°C	27°C	31°C	31°C	30°C	26°C	28°C	9°C	3°C
34°F	39°F	51°F	70°F	81°F	88°F	88°F	86°F	79°F	82°F	48°F	37°F

🔅 High season 🔅 Low season

Temperatures listed are the average daily maximum in Beijing. China's climate varies massively from region to region. Deepest winter can be bitterly cold and summer is often witheringly hot – both seasons should be avoided if possible. Beijing is extremely cold in winter and very hot in summer. Shanghai has a mild winter but an extremely hot and humid summer. Hong Kong is invariably warm and sticky, but cools off over the winter months. Only Yunnan, in southwest China, has a genuinely pleasant year-round climate. Summer is probably the least pleasant time to travel in China, because of the temperatures and the crowds. If you can bear the chill, there's much to recommend travelling in late autumn or early winter. Avoid Chinese New Year holidays (January/February), Labour Day holidays (first week of May) and National Day holidays (first week of October).

WHAT YOU NEED

● Required
○ Suggested
▲ Not required

Contact your travel agent or the U.S. embassy for the current regulations regarding passports and the Visa Waiver Form/Visa. Your passport should be valid for at lest six months beyond date of entry.

	UK	Germany	USA	Netherlands	Spain
Passport/National Identity Card (Valid for 6 months after entry)	●	●	●	●	●
Visa	●	●	●	●	●
Onward or Return Ticket	○	○	○	○	○
Health Inoculations	○	○	○	○	○
Health Documentation (► 23, Health)	▲	▲	▲	▲	▲
Travel Insurance	○	○	○	○	○
Driving Licence (national or International Driving Permit)	N/A	N/A	N/A	N/A	N/A
Car Insurance Certificate	N/A	N/A	N/A	N/A	N/A

WEBSITES

www.cnta.gov.cn/lyen
www.cnto.org
www.english.bjta.gov.cn

www.lyw.sh.gov.cn/en
www.discoverhongkong.com
www.en.beijing-2008.org

TOURIST OFFICES AT HOME

In the UK

CNTO (China National Tourist Office)
71 Warwick Road
London SW5 9HB
☎ (020) 7373 0888

In the USA

CNTO 350 Fifth Avenue, Suite 6413
Empire State Building
New York, NY 10118
☎ (1 888) 760 8218

HEALTH INSURANCE

All visitors are strongly recommended to arrange medical insurance
before leaving for China; this should include transport home. Medical
facilities are good. Most tourist hotels should be able to recommend a
good dental clinic. Any treatment will need to be paid for in advance and
then reclaimed on insurance.

Immunisation Typhoid, hepatitis A, diphtheria and rabies are all potential
issues in China and anyone concerned should seek medical advice prior to
travel. Malaria is present only in parts of Guangdong, Hainan and Yunnan
and, assuming you are limiting your travel to major tourist areas and big
cities, there's little to fear.

TIME DIFFERENCES

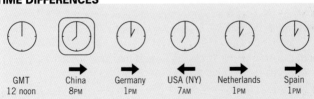

GMT	China	Germany	USA (NY)	Netherlands	Spain
12 noon	8PM	1PM	7AM	1PM	1PM

China is eight hours ahead of Greenwich Mean Time (GMT+8). The whole
country officially lies within the same time zone, though Xinjiang, in the far
west, operates local hours two hours behind Beijing Standard Time.
Daylight saving time is not used, meaning China is seven hours ahead
during the summer.

NATIONAL HOLIDAYS

1 Jan *New Year's Day*

Jan/Feb *Chinese New Year (7 days)**

8 March *International Women's Day*

1–7 May *Labour Day Holiday*

1 June *International Children's Day*

1 July *Birthday of the Chinese Communist Party*

1 August *People's Liberation Army Day*

Sep/Oct *Mid-Autumn Festival**

1–7 Oct *National Day Holiday*

*Governed by the lunar calendar

WHAT'S ON WHEN

January/February *Chinese Lunar New Year:* the most important holiday of the year for the Chinese begins on the first day of the lunar calendar's first moon and lasts for seven consecutive days. Families come together to enjoy special meals and to light fireworks, and lively temple fairs are held in major parks. Some shops and restaurants may operate limited working hours or even close, especially in more remote areas. However, most urban centres will remain busy. Indeed, shopping and eating are two of the most popular leisure activities for families during this holiday.

Lantern Festival: this popular celebration, marking the end of the Spring Festival, falls on the 15th day of the first lunar month. People buy paper lanterns and walk through parks and streets with them illuminated.

The Tibetan Lunar New Year: falls in January, February or, occasionally, March and is marked by archery and horseback competitions, religious dances and other ceremonies.

Guanyin's Birthday: marks the birthday of Guanyin, Buddhism's Goddess of Mercy, on the 19th day of the second moon.

April *Qingming (Tomb Sweeping) Festival:* traditional holiday when Chinese tidy and decorate the burial places of their ancestors.

Water Splashing Festival of the Dai Nationality: this 'minority' festival takes place 13–15 April in Xishuangbanna, southern Yunnan province, and involves dragon-boat races, fireworks and water fights.

May *May Day Holiday (1–7 May):* International Labour Day is now celebrated in China as a week-long holiday. This is not a good time to travel in China, as travel and hotels can be difficult to reserve.

May/June *Dragon Boat Festival (May/June):* commemorates the death of Qu Yuan, a patriot and poet who drowned himself as an act of political protest. The day is marked by dragon-boat races and the consumption of zongzi; bamboo leaves stuffed with sticky rice and a meat or bean filling. *Children's Day (1 June):* teachers, parents and children go to parks and on field trips.

August/September *Mid-Autumn Festival (15th day of the 8th moon):* celebrates a 14th-century uprising against the Mongols. People present friends with Mooncakes, and gather outside to stare at the heavens.

October *National Day Holiday (1–7 October):* commemorates the founding of the People's Republic of China. The government has designated this week-long holiday designed to encourage domestic tourism and spending. It's probably the worst time to travel in China.

Event Listings For up-to-date information on where to eat, shop and play in Beijing, Shanghai and Guangzhou check out *City Weekend* (www.cityweekend.com.cn), a free bi-weekly English magazine. The monthly series of 'That's' magazines (www.thatsmags.com) are also good sources of information on Beijing, Shanghai, Guangzhou and Shenzen, and areavailable from hotels, bars and restaurants. Also useful is www.xianzai.com, offering weekly listings of events.

Getting there

BY AIR

Beijing Capital International Airport		
25km (15.5 miles) to city centre	🚆	16 minutes
	🚌	40 minutes
	🚕	30 minutes

Pudong International Airport		
40km (25 miles) to city centre	🚆	8 minutes
	🚌	50 minutes
	🚕	40 minutes

Hong Kong International Airport		
40km (25 miles) to city centre	🚆	22 minutes
	🚌	50 minutes
	🚕	40 minutes

Beijing Capital International Airport (www.bcia.com.cn) has six major Airport Bus routes (7am–11pm) into the city. By 2008 an elevated railway will connect the airport with the existing city centre metro. A taxi ride to the north of the city can cost as little as 50RMB.

All long-haul international flights to Shanghai land at Pudong International Airport (www.shanghaiairport.com). There are seven main

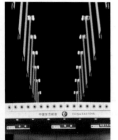

Airport Bus routes into the city (7:30am–11pm). The Maglev (Magnetic Levitation train) whisks passengers the 30km (19 miles) to Longyang Lu metro station in eight minutes (7am–9pm). Taxis to the city centre cost around 140RMB.

Hong Kong International Airport (www.hongkongairport.com) is located around 40km (25 miles) from Hong Kong Island. Buses, trains and taxis make the trip, though the Airport Express train is the most convenient method, speeding to Kowloon or Hong Kong Island (Central) in around 20 minutes.

BY TRAIN

It's possible to arrive in mainland China by train via several routes. The Trans-Siberian from Moscow crosses the Russia-China border at Manzhouli, in Inner Mongolia, before stopping at Harbin and Beijing.

The Trans-Mongolian enters China at Erenhot, also in Inner Mongolia, before heading onto Beijing. The only other international link is with Hanoi. There are twice-weekly services from Beijing to the Vietnamese capital, though a change of train is required at the Vietnam-China border. In all cases, customs formalities are completed at the border and passengers are required to disembark.

Hong Kong has direct train links with the mainland along three routes, Beijing, Shanghai and the Guangdong city of Zhaoqing (stopping at Guangzhou en route). The trains pass directly through the Hong Kong-China border and customs formalities are completed on arrival.

Getting around

PUBLIC TRANSPORT

Internal flights Planes are more expensive than trains but, when converted back to your own currency, the difference is often negligible. You will find that some provincial governments also run their own airlines.

Trains China's rail network is excellent and is the country's main means of transportation. There are soft sleeper berths (four people sharing a cabin) and hard sleeper berths (six people sharing a section in an open car).

Buses Bus services are widely used within and between towns and cities, although the quality and comfort varies sharply. Buses are generally viewed as less safe as highway conditions are often poor, seat belts are scarce and traffic can be chaotic.

Ferries There are ferry services from Hong Kong to Guangzhou and Shanghai. The trip to Guangzhou takes 12 hours on the overnight ship, or four hours on jetfoils. The trip to Shanghai is three days. There are ferry services along the Yangzi River, and between cities on the east coast. You can take a tourist boat along the Grand Canal, from Hangzhou to Suzhou.

FARES AND TICKETS

Trains Obtaining train tickets is difficult in China. Depending on the route, tickets only become available between three and seven days prior to departure. It's cheapest to buy tickets at the station but the crowds are heavy. For a surcharge, you can buy tickets through your hotel. In smaller cities tickets must be booked at the point of departure.

Air Though travel agents can help buy tickets it's possible to book cheaply online using web-based aggregators (www.ctrip.com or www.elong.com). International credit cards can often be used, though there are sometimes problems processing payment.

Buses and ferries Tickets are generally plentiful and can easily be booked from the depature point.

TAXIS

Taxis are cheap and convenient. Few drivers speak English, so it's advisable to have your destination written in Chinese, and to always carry a business card from your hotel with its address in Chinese. Patronize only taxis from the line in front of the main doors of the airport terminal.

DRIVING

- Speed limits on intercity expressways: 120kph (75mph); on urban express roads: 100kph (62mph); on urban roads: 70kph (43mph); on single-lane urban roads: 30kph (19mph).
- Conditions on Chinese roads seem chaotic to outsiders. The concept of Right of Way doesn't exist and it's common for drivers to pull out in front of oncoming vehicles. Expect the unexpected at all times.
- It's compulsory for drivers and passengers to wear seat belts on highways, though this is rarely enforced.
- Breaches of the rules often go unpunished, although if a driver is stopped, offences will usually be punished with a fine.

CAR RENTAL

Renting your own car is only possible in Beijing, Shanghai, Hong Kong and Macau, but you are only allowed to drive within the city's boundaries. Taking taxis remains a cheaper and easier option for many of China's visitors. It's possible to hire a car with a driver for trips outside the city to scenic spots. New rules making it easier for foreign license holders to obtain a temporary Chinese Driving License are being discussed, though these have yet to come into force.

Being there

TOURIST OFFICES

Beijing and Shanghai have a network of government-sponsored centers, as well as dedicated tourism 'hotlines'. However, the quality of information and levels of English are often poor.

Beijing There are several information centres throughout the city.
Beijing Tourism Hotline ☎ 010 6513 0828; www.english.bjta.gov.cn/btic.

Shanghai There are several information centres dotted around the city.
Shanghai Tourist Hotline ☎ 021 6355 5032; www.lyw.sh.gov.cn/en/info.

Hong Kong Hong Kong has superb tourism information facilities.
There are Hong Kong Tourism Board information counters at Hong Kong International Airport. There is also a multi-lingual tourist information hotline: ☎ 852 2508 1234; www.discoverhongkong.com.

MONEY

The renminbi (RMB) is the main unit of currency in China. It's also known as the yuan and referred to in speech as 'kuai'. It is divided into 10 jiao. Notes are in denominations of 1, 2, 5, 10, 20, 50 and 100RMB. The Hong Kong dollar (HK$) is the currency of Hong Kong and the pataca (MOP) is the currency of Macau. All three currencies are roughly equal in value, though the renmimbi is maginally the strongest and the pataca weakest.

Major credit cards are accepted in many places in China's larger cities and most airports and city banks have facilities for changing foreign currency and travellers' cheques. It's possible to obtain cash from nearly all Bank of China ATM machines using international debit cards.

TIPS

It is useful to carry plenty of small notes		
Yes ✓ No ✗		
Restaurants (if service not included)	✗	
Bar Service	✗	
Taxis	✗	
Tour guides	✓	5–10RMB per day
Hotels (chambermaid/doorman etc)	✗	
Porters	✓	5RMB
Hairdressers	✗	
Toilets	✗	

Tipping is officially discouraged in China, but tour guides and staff at hotels who carry bags will often expect a small tip. Some restaurants may include a 10–15 per cent service charge in the bill.

POSTAL AND INTERNET SERVICES

Post offices Times vary, though 9am–5pm, Mon–Sun, is a rough guide. The airmail rate for postcards is 4RMB. Airmailed letters cost around 5RMB to Europe, USA and Canada, though the price depends on weight.

Internet services China has become as extremely wired nation in recent years. Most hotels offer Internet access though prices are relatively expensive. Dark and smoky Internet cafés infest China's towns and cities though finding them can be tricky and most are not signed in English. Look out for shopfront pictures of cartoon characters or fantasy warriors.

Prices costs from as little as 2RMB per hour. Coffee shops in bigger cities often have complimentary computers and many offer free wireless access for those with laptops.

TELEPHONES

Public telephones are hard to find sometimes. Calls cost 50 fen for a local call. IP cards can be purchased at newspaper booths for long-distance calls.

International dialling codes
Dial 00 followed by:
UK: 44
USA/Canada: 1
Irish Republic: 353
France: 33
Germany: 49

The dialling code for mainland China is 86 (applies from Hong Kong or Macau)
The dialling code for Hong Kong is 852 (applies from the mainland)
The dialling code for Macau is 853 (applies from the mainland)

Emergency telephone numbers
Police: 110   Fire: 119   Ambulance: 120

EMBASSIES AND CONSULATES

UK ☎ (010) 8529 6600   Netherlands ☎ (010) 8532 0200
Germany ☎ (010) 8532 9000   Spain ☎ (010) 6532 3629
USA ☎ (010) 6532 3831

HEALTH ADVICE

Sun advice Central and southern China can be hot and sticky, while the north is extremely dry. It is easy to become dehydrated. It's also easy to burn at higher altitudes in western China, especially Tibet.

Drugs Pharmacies sell much of the same range of everyday medicines you would find in Western Europe or America but they are rarely labelled in English. There are English-speaking pharmacists at some clinics in the larger cities, but prices for medicine at foreign clinics can be steep.

Safe water Tap water in China is not safe to drink and must be boiled before drinking. Bottled water is widely available at restaurants, small shops and kiosks. It is not advisable to walk barefoot in rice paddies or other wet areas.

PLANNING

ELECTRICITY

China's power supply is 220 volts. Plugs come in a variety of sizes. Plugs come in a variety of shapes, and most sockets accept at least two varieties. Most modern plugs are two-pin, similar to those used in the USA. Hong Kong uses the same three-pin plugs as the UK.

PERSONAL SAFETY

China is relatively safe, and although theft is rare, you are advised to take the usual precautions. Pickpockets are common on crowded city streets and on buses, so place your passport and wallet in a safe place. In public places keep a close watch on your bags and other valuables. There is a lot of counterfeit money in circulation in China, so do not change currency with money exchangers on the street.

OPENING HOURS

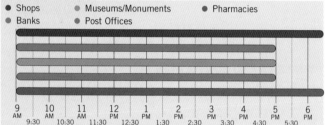

- Shops
- Banks
- Museums/Monuments
- Post Offices
- Pharmacies

9 AM · 9:30 · 10 AM · 10:30 · 11 AM · 11:30 · 12 PM · 12:30 · 1 PM · 1:30 · 2 PM · 2:30 · 3 PM · 3:30 · 4 PM · 4:30 · 5 PM · 5:30 · 6 PM

Department stores open around 10am and usually close at 10pm. Markets open as early as 3am and are finished by 8am, others stay open later. Hong Kong shops may not open until 11am but generally stay open very late. Banks open daily, though some services may not be available during the long lunch break (11:30am–2:30pm) and on weekends.

LANGUAGE

On the whole few Chinese speak English, although many will be enthuastic to speak to you. Chinese characters are rendered into the Latin alphabet by an official system known as pinyin. Most sounds are composed of an intial and a final. Sounds are largely pronounced as written, but note the following:

Initials c as the 'ts' is cats; j as the 'j' in 'jeep' but slightly sharper; q as the 'ch' in cheap but slightly sharper; r has no English equivalent and is pronounced as a cross between y and r; x as the 'sh' in sheep but with the s given greater emphasis; z as the 'ds' in lids; zh as 'j' in jam.

Finals a as the 'ar' in car; e as the 'er' in her; er as 'are' in are, with a vocalised final r; i as 'ee' in feet unless preceded by c, ch, r, s, sh, z, zh when it is pronounced as the 'er' in her, but with no exhalation; o as 'war' in war; u as the 'oo' in cool; ai as 'y' in sky; ei as 'ay' in play; ao as 'ow' in cow; ou as as 'o' in so; en as 'un' in under; ie as 'ye' in yes; ia as 'ya' in yard; un as 'on' in won.

hotel	*fan dian*	how much is it?	*duo shao qian?*
guest house	*bing guan*	room	*fang jian*
do you have a room?	*ni you mei you fang jian?*	bathroom	*xi shou jian*
		toilet	*ce suo*

how much is this?	*zhe ge shi duo shao qian?*	3	*san*	10	*shi*
		4	*si*	11	*shi yi*
too expensive	*tai gui*	5	*wu*	20	*er shi*
inexpensive	*bu gui/pian yi*	6	*liu*	30	*san shi*
0	*ling*	7	*qi*	100	*yi bai*
1	*yi*	8	*ba*	1,000	*yi qian*
2	*er*	9	*jiu*		

rice	*fan*	pork	*zhu rou*
noodles	*mian tiao*	shrimp	*xia*
fried rice	*chao fan*	soup	*tang*
egg	*ji dan*	fruit	*shui guo*
fish	*yu*	boiled water	*kai shui*
duck	*ya*	tea	*cha*
chicken	*ji rou*	coffee	*ka fei*
beef	*niu rou*	beer	*pi jiu*

aeroplane	*fei ji*	railway station	*huo che zhan*
airport	*fei ji chang*	taxi	*chu zu che*
bus	*gong gong qi che*	bicycle	*zi xing che*
bus station	*gong gong qi che zhan*	I would like to go...	*wo yao qu*
		Where is the...?	*...zai nar?*
train	*huo che*	I would like a ticket	*wo yao mai piao*

hello	*ni hao?*	I don't understand	*wo bu dong*
goodbye	*zai jian*	Do you understand?	*ni dong bu dong?*
How are you?	*ni hao ma?*	yes	*shi*
Well, thank you.	*hen hao, xie xie*	no	*bu shi*
thank you	*xie xie*	I like...	*wo xi huan*
When?	*shen me shi hou?*	I don't like...	*wo bu xi huan*
No problem	*mei you wen ti*	today	*jin tian*
What is this?	*zhe ge shi shen me?*	yesterday	*ming tian*
I understand	*wo dong*	tomorrow	*zuo tian*

Best places to see

1 Bingmayong (Terracotta Warriors)

During a drought in 1974, farmers digging a well discovered one of the most amazing archaeological finds in modern history – the terracotta warriors.

The terracotta army – thousands of soldiers, horses and chariots – had remained secretly on duty for some 2,000 years, guarding the nearby mausoleum of Qin Shi Huang, the first emperor of the Qin Dynasty. Known as the Huangdi, or Yellow Emperor, Qin ruled from 221–206BC and is credited for unifying China for the first time. He's also remembered for his ruthless destruction of books and slaughter of his enemies.

Each of the terracotta figures – some standing, some on horseback, and some kneeling, bows drawn – is unique, with a different hairstyle and facial expression. Three pits have already been dug at the site in Lintong county, 37km (23 miles) east of Xi'an. Pit No 1 is home to about 6,000 life-size terracotta figurines in a military formation marching east. Pit No 2 contains hundreds of chariot drivers, horses, cavalrymen and infantrymen. Pit No 3 is thought to be the army headquarters.

Qin's mausoleum lies 1.5km (1 mile) to the east of the terracotta warriors, and it is believed that a larger terracotta army and valuable cultural relics lay buried in the tomb. Hu Hai, the second Qin Emperor, reputedly mandated the sacrificial burial of

all the builders and childless imperial maids. Visitors are able to walk around the site, but it has yet to be excavated due to the construction methods used to build the tomb, which make it impossible to safely excavate using current techniques.

➕ 2F ✉ Shaanxi Province, 37km (23 miles) from Xi'an 🕐 Mar–Nov daily 8:30–5:30; Dec–Feb 8:30–5 💰 Moderate

🚌 Buses from Xi'an Railway Station and Xi'an Bus Terminal 🚉 Xi'an Station
✈ Xi'an International Airport

2 Changcheng (The Great Wall)

One of mankind's greatest achievements, the Great Wall was built between the 5th century BC and AD 16th century.

The Great Wall was originally built to keep out barbarian invaders from the north and stretches 5,900km (3,658 miles) from the Bohai Gulf to Jiayuguan in the mountains of Gansu Province. While the bulk of the wall is now in ruins, some sections have been repaired in recent years.

The Ming rulers paid great attention to the care of the wall. As a result, much of the wall in northeast China today dates back to this period. Despite the Ming's dedication, the Manchu tribes who overthrew them poured through an opening in the wall at its eastern terminus in 1644 when the Ming general Wu Sangui defected to the Manchu side, leaving the Shanhai Pass unguarded.

The most accessible sites for tourists are Badaling and Mutianyu. These are also the most commercial and crowded sections of the wall.

The best views can be found at Simatai and Jinshanling, a slightly longer drive from the capital, where less restoration work has been carried out, and where fewer tourists venture. There are also cable cars at Badaling, Simatai and Mutianyu for those visitors who have trouble negotiating the steep steps.

🚩 1E–5D 🖂 Badaling, Yanqing county; Jinshanling, Miyun county; Mutianyu, Huairou county; Simatai, Miyun county
☎ Badaling (010) 6912 2222; Mutianyu (010) 6162 6505; Simatai (010) 6903 1051
👜 Moderate 🍴 Restaurants at entrance points ($–$$) 🚌 Badaling: Buses from Qianmen, Beijing Railway Station, Dongdaqiao and Andingmen, weekends. Mutianyu: No 6 bus from Xuanwumen or Dongsi Shitiao. Simatai: No 12 bus from Dongsi Shitiao or Xuanwumen
🚆 Badaling: 623 from Beijing Station

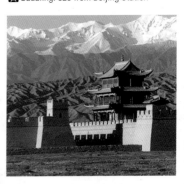

3 Chang Jiang (Yangtze River)

Rising in the icy mountains of Qinghai Province, the Yangtze passes through seven provinces, ending its journey in the East China Sea close to Shanghai.

The Yangtze, at 6,380km (3,956 miles) in length, is the third longest river in the world, dividing China between the wheat-growing north and the rice-growing south. Every turn of the river brings to mind stories from history and mythology, such as Kublai Khan's crossing of the river on his conquest of the Song dynasty in the 13th century.

Most Yangtze cruises begin at Chongqing and head downriver in the direction of the Three Gorges Dam. Many of the towns once visited by the cruise ships are now under

water thanks to the reservoir created by the dam. The river was first dammed across its entire width in 2003 and the Yangtze has been on the rise ever since. By the time the high watermark is reached in 2008, the Yangtze's

famous Three Gorges will be 105m (114yds) shorter than previously.

The gorges, located on a 200km (124 miles) length of the river between Baidicheng and Yichang, are crowded with towering peaks, jagged cliffs and caves. Qutang is the shortest, but most beautiful, of the three. Wu, or Sorceress Gorge, is surrounded by sloping forests and strange mountain peaks. Xiling, the last and longest, is marked by shoals and rapids.

At 'New' Wushan travellers can disembark for an excursion through the Three Lesser Gorges of the Daning River, riding the waters through almost surreal scenery.

Approaching Yichang, the cruise boats pass through the five colossal locks of the Three Gorges Project. Once you reach the other side, it's possible to climb atop the dam, 185m (607ft) high. Yichang is now the stopping point for most river cruises.

✚ 1H–5G ✉ Central China

🍴 Cruise ships serve food ⛴ Boats from Chongqing to Yichang (3 days, 2 nights)

❓ Tours can be arranged through the China International Travel Service (CITS) and international travel agencies. Note that a variety of boats can be booked, from simple steamers to expensive cruise ships.

4 Gugong (Forbidden City)

www.dpm.org.cn

Established between 1406 and 1420, the Forbidden City remains the most complete collection of imperial architecture in China.

With around 9,000 rooms, the Imperial Palace (Forbidden City) is the largest palace complex in the world. It was home to China's emperors from 1420 to 1911. During this time the palace was rebuilt many times, but always retained its original design. The wall that surrounds the complex, anchored at the corners by four guard towers, is encircled by a moat. The palace is divided into three sections: the palace gates, principal halls and inner court.

After passing through the Gate of Heavenly Peace (Tiananmen) and the Upright Gate you reach the Meridian Gate, the traditional entrance to the Forbidden City. Only the emperor was permitted to enter here. Beyond this is the final portal, the Gate of Supreme Harmony.

The outer courtyard was designed to accommodate 90,000 people during ceremonies. In the centre stands the Hall of Supreme Harmony. Important ceremonies were held here, including the emperor's birthday. Behind this stand the Hall of Complete Harmony, where the emperor dressed for functions, and the Hall of Preserving Harmony. Within the inner courtyard the Palace of Heavenly Purity, Hall of Heavenly and Terrestrial Union and Palace of Terrestrial Tranquillity were used for lesser functions. The Palace of Terrestrial Tranquillity was where the emperors consummated their marriages. The smaller courts in the east and west are where the imperial families, concubines and attendants lived. Behind this can be found the Imperial Garden.

✚ *Beijing 5c* ✉ Xichangan Jie, Beijing
☎ (010) 8511 7311 🕓 Apr–Oct daily 8:30am–5pm; Nov–Mar daily 8:30am–4:30pm 💷 Moderate
🍴 Starbucks café southeast of the Hall of Preserving Harmony at southern entrance ($) 🚇 Tiananmen East or Tiananmen West 🚌 1, 2, 4, 10, 20, 52, 57, 101

5 Hong Kong

A British colony from 1841 until it was returned to China in 1997, Hong Kong is the ultimate example of East meets West.

Hong Kong is a bustling city of contrasts where glistening skyscrapers dwarf small temples and bustling produce markets. Cross Victoria Harbour on the Star Ferry for a spectacular view of the skyline. Outside the Star Ferry Terminal (Pier 7) in Central, board the 15C bus to the Peak Tram Station for the steep vertical ascent to Victoria Peak. Once on the Peak you can enjoy a bird's-eye view of the harbour and city below and then take a gentle stroll along one of the surrounding paths. The view is stunning and well worth it, though air pollution often blurs the view during daylight hours. Jump on a double-decker bus (get a seat on the upper deck if you can) for the spectacular roller-coaster ride to Stanley where you can browse colourful market stalls or walk along the beach. Visit one of the floating seafood restaurants in Aberdeen for some delicious and fresh seafood.

The 'Heritage Tour' will take you to the area between the Kowloon Hills and mainland China, a diverse rural and suburban region where you will visit traditional temples, homes, markets and a picturesque walled village. A 40-minute ferry ride will whisk you from the booming Central district to one of the many serene offshore islands where you'll see fishermen

patiently tending their nets and farmers working in the fields.

Head to Lantau Island to visit the Po Lin Monastery, home of a huge seated Buddha. Stay for a vegetarian lunch at the temple and then visit the nearby fishing village of Tai O. Or for a more active option take a ride out to Lamma Island and walk along small paths past old farmhouses and up into the hills for spectacular sea views. Finish your visit with an inexpensive seafood meal by the water as the sun goes down.

✚ 3L ✉ Southern China

🚇 Mass Transit Railway (MRT) links all districts

🚌 Bus and tram services

🚆 Kowloon–Canton Railway (KCT) ⛴ Star Ferry

❓ The Heritage Tour is run by the Hong Kong Tourist Board (852) 2508 1234.

6 Lhasa

The spiritual, cultural and political centre of Tibet. All devout Tibetan Buddhists hope to make a pilgrimage to this holy city at least once.

The Potala Palace is the largest and most complete palace complex in Tibet. It was built in the seventh century, but was destroyed by war in the ninth century. The present structure, located on a hill overlooking Lhasa, was built in 1645 by the fifth Dalai Lama. It is divided into two sections, the White and Red Palaces. The White Palace, built in 1653, is where Dalai Lamas administered government affairs. In 1690, eight years after the death of the fifth Dalai Lama, a local regent decided to build a funerary pagoda to house his remains, and work was begun on the Red Palace. This palace, located between the eastern and western wings of the White Palace, is decorated with a gilded copper roof, and includes chapels, shrines and the tombs of former Dalai Lamas. The inner room of the present Dalai Lama's apartment has been left just as it was on the day he fled to India in 1959, moments before the People's Liberation Army arrived to reinforce Chinese rule over Tibet. Paintings are an important part of the palace, consisting of murals, thankga, or Tibetan painted scrolls, and other decorations.

The nearby Jokhang Temple is always crowded with pilgrims and is famous as the home of one of the most precious Buddhist images in China, the

Sakyamuni Buddha. The statue was brought here from China by Wen Cheng, a Tang dynasty princess who married the Tibetan King Songsten Gampo. The main hall has a set of murals portraying Princess Wen Cheng's arrival in Tibet.

🕂 10R ✉ Provincial capital of Tibet

🕐 The Potala: daily 9–4. Jokhang Temple: daily 9–5

🍴 Restaurants throughout Lhasa ($) 🚌 Buses and minibuses cover the city ✈ Flights from Beijing, Chengdu, Chongqing and Xi'an ❓ All foreign visitors need a Tibetan Travel Permit to enter Tibet

7 Lijiang

Nestled in the lee of the snow-capped Jade Dragon Mountain, Lijiang, with its traditional architecture and ancient canals, is the best-preserved old town in China.

Lijiang is one of the few towns in China to survive the wrecking ball that has transformed much of the rest of the country. Old wooden houses with tiled roofs face the thick cobblestone streets. Canals criss-cross the town, accented here and there by quaint stone bridges. At intervals, steps descend to the surface of the water where indigineous Naxi

housewives wash laundry or vegetables in the cold clear streams.

Lijiang, one of 33 UNESCO World Heritage Sites in China, is divided into two parts. The old town, which has not changed much in recent decades, is the place to visit. The brick and timber structures are marked by falling eaves and wooden slats carved with various auspicious symbols. The fronts of the houses are covered by ornately carved panelled wooden doors. However, the rows of beautiful old shops have traded their traditional wares for souvenirs. Chinese restaurants sell traditional delicacies next to Western coffee-houses serving burgers, fries, milkshakes and brownies. If you want to beat the crowds, lose yourself in the fascinating alleyways behind the main streets, or head up into the hills for panoramic views.

Naxi society was traditionally shamanistic and structured along matriarchal lines. The Naxi have unique music and dance traditions, which add to the town's rich cultural *mélange*. Local musicians can often be heard performing the ancient music of Lijiang, which is believed to be a form of Taoist music that spread here in the Song Dynasty. The Naxi are also known for their unique written language, one of the last pictographic scripts in existance today.

✚ 12S ✉ Yunnan Province, 196km (122 miles) from Dali
🍴 Small Chinese and Western restaurants are scattered throughout the town ($–$$) 🚌 No vehicles are allowed in the old city, which can be easily covered on foot. Buses for Lijiang can be taken from Kunming and Dali
✈ Daily scheduled flights leave from Kunming. There are also direct flights from Chongqing, Chengdu and Shenzhen.

8 Mogao Ku (Mogao Caves)

The Mogao Grottoes of Dunhuang house a rich collection of Buddhist sculptures and frescoes.

In the Han dynasty, Dunhuang was an important Buddhist centre because of its position at the junction of the northern and southern tracks of the Silk Road. It was under Tibetan control from 781 to 847, when there was an intense rivalry for control of the trading routes across Central Asia. The caves date from the fourth century, and the site is among

the most impressive along the Silk Road. It's said that a Buddhist monk had a vision in which he saw 1,000 Buddhas. He began to carve grottoes into the sandstone cliff, and was later joined by other monks and craftsmen, who filled the caves with Buddhist images.

There were originally up to 1,000 caves, of which 492 still survive, filled with about 2,400 clay statues. Murals dating back to the Northern Wei Dynasty show the strong influence of Central Asian Buddhist traditions. Of special significance is cave 17, which houses a huge collection of paintings, manuscripts and textiles spanning six centuries. It provides invaluable evidence for the history and development of Chinese art. However, as tourism takes its toll, the number of caves open to the public is dwindling.

✚ 11P ✉ 25km (15.5 miles) southeast of Dunhuang, Gansu Province 🕐 Daily 8–5 ✋ Expensive

🚌 Buses from Dunhuang. Hotels also arrange transportation 🚆 Trains on the Lanzhou-Urumqi line stop at Liuyuan (also known as Dunhuang), where buses depart for Dunhuang city ✈ Dunhuang Airport

❓ Visitors must be accompanied by a tour guide (included in the ticket price). Photography is strictly forbidden in the caves. Bring your own torch, or rent one at the entrance.

Qingdao

Qingdao still retains charming traces of its brief encounter with Europe.

Qingdao, or Green Island, is one of the most beautiful port cities in China. The city was just a small fishing village until Europeans began to take an interest in it in the mid-19th century. The Russians made it their winter anchorage in 1895, and the Germans turned it into a foreign concession in 1897, using the murder of two Catholic missionaries as a pretext. The Germans gave the city a makeover during their 17-year rule, building Bavarian-style mansions, churches and a train station. Qingdao was then divided into European, Chinese and business districts. The town was given to the Japanese under the Treaty of Versailles in 1919, but was finally returned to China in 1922.

A walk through the streets of the former German Quarter and residential neighbourhoods reveals the city's German heritage. Huaishilou, a castle-like structure, once served as the German governor's residence. The double-spired Catholic church, near Zhongshan Road, and the Protestant church, opposite Xinhaoshan Park, are excellent examples of German architecture, as is the Bavarian-style Xinhaoshan Hotel, which is adjacent to the park.

One of the city's most famous institutions is the Tsingtao Brewery (this is the older spelling of the city's name). The brewery was founded in 1903 by the Germans, and continues today to brew its distinct German recipe in the original copper stills.

Qingdao is also known for its six beaches and fresh seafood – an ever-prominent part of Shandong cuisine.

➕ 5E ✉ Shandong Province 🍴 Street stalls on Zhongshan Lu ($) 🚌 No 6 bus covers most of the city's major sites 🚉 Qingdao Railway Station 🚢 Boats to Shanghai and Inchon, South Korea ✈ Qingdao Airport

❓ Beer Festival, August

10 Yangshuo

With its amazing karst formations, Yangshuo is like falling into a Chinese landscape painting.

In recent years Yangshuo has become a mecca for foreign tourists, lured by the unique beauty of the surrounding countryside. The best way to explore the area is by bicycle, passing bamboo groves, orange orchards, cinnamon trees, and fields of sugar cane, peanuts, watermelons and tobacco. Moon Hill, a limestone peak marked by a moon-shaped hole, is a bike ride 10km (6 miles)

southwest of Yangshuo. A 30-minute hike to the top provides excellent views of the surrounding countryside.

Boat tours out of Yangshuo are available and travel upriver to Xingping, or downstream to Fuli. Xingping is known for its beautiful natural scenery. In addition to amazing views, Fuli is a small fishing and farming village with traditional architecture and narrow streets. You can also hire your own small boat for a leisurely trip down the Li River, getting off to explore rustic villages where fishing is still practised with tamed cormorants.

Back in Yangshuo, cobblestoned Xi Jie, or West Street, has a wide array of souvenir shops to browse selling a variety of arts and crafts. Diecui Road is a good place for a look at a local produce market and to mingle with locals. For those in need of a brief break from China, dine outside at one of the bar-cum-restaurants which serve up inexpensive Western dishes. These restaurants and coffee shops offer value for money and are good places to get advice on touring the area.

➕ 2K ✉ 65km (40 miles) south of Guilin, Guangxi Province 🍴 Chinese and Western restaurants on main street ($) 🚌 Buses from Guilin, Liuzhou and Guangzho 🚉 Guilin Railway Station 🚢 Li River Cruise ($$–$$$) ✈ Guilin Airport

Best things to do

Great places to have lunch

King Roast Duck Restaurant ($$)
Traditional Peking roast duck cooked in fruit-wood heated ovens.
✉ 24 Jianguomenwai Dajie, Beijing ☎ (010) 6515 6908

Lao Hanzi ($$)
The hearty dishes of China's Hakka minority served on the scenic
banks of Shichahai.
✉ 12 Shichahai Dong'an (close to Ping'an Dadao), Beijing ☎ (010) 6404 2259

South Silk Road (Chama Gudao) ($$)
Spicy, earthy Yunnan food served in a hip restaurant.
✉ 3rd Floor, Building D, Soho (Xiandaicheng), 500m (545yds) west of Guomao
metro station on Dong Chang'an Jie, Beijing ☎ (010) 8580 4286

Yang's Kitchen ($$)
Shanghai-style cooking in home-like surroundings.
✉ No 3, Alley 9 Hengshan Lu, Shanghai ☎ (021) 6445 8418

M on the Bund ($$$)
Excellent Western cuisine served up with one of the most beautiful views of the Bund.
✉ 7th Floor, 20 Guangdong Lu, Shanghai ☎ (021) 6350 9988; www.m-restaurantgroup.com

Chen Mapo Doufu Dian ($)
Home of Sichuan's famous spicy mapo doufu and a wide variety of other popular Sichuan snacks.
✉ 197 Xiyulong Jie, Chengdu, Sichuan ☎ (028) 8675 4512

Sakura Café ($)
Good Western, Chinese, Korean and Japanese food is served up at this Korean-run restaurant, with outdoor seating along a beautiful section of the canal.
✉ 123 Cuiwenduan, Xinhua Lu, Old Town, Lijiang, Yunnan
☎ (0888) 518 7619

Laosun Jia ($$)
Popular Shaanxi and Muslim dishes, including the famous *yangrou paomo*, bread and lamb cooked in a tasty broth.
✉ 364 Dongda Jie, Xi'an, Shaanxi ☎ (026) 8721 4438

The Sampan ($$$)
Enjoy fresh seafood al fresco overlooking the picturesque Lamma Harbour. Dim sum is served in the mornings.
✉ Main Street, Yung Shue Wan, Lamma Island, Hong Kong
☎ (852) 2982 2388

Pousada De Sao Tigao Macau ($$$)
Tasty Portuguese cuisine overlooking the Pearl River. This hotel is the former Fortaleza da Barra, a fortress built in the 17th century.
✉ Avenida da Republica, Fortaleza de Sao Tiago da Barra, Macau
☎ (853) 28378 111

Top activities

Walking: explore Beijing's *hutongs*, old alleyways lined with traditional houses.

Taijiquan (Tai Chi Ch'uan): an ancient slow form of Chinese exercise that is often practised early in the morning.

Ballroom dancing: outdoor activity that takes place either early morning or in the evening in parks and squares.

Museum hopping: visit some of the museums showcasing Chinese history and culture.

Karaoke: hugely popular evening entertainment option among locals.

Shopping: for local products and handicrafts in local markets.

Birdwatching: in the spring and autumn in Beidaihe on the northeast coast of China.

Cycling: still the way many Chinese get around, and a good way to see the city. Bicycle rentals available at most hotels.

Visit a park: walk around the city parks, watching Chinese hard at play.

Fly a kite: buy a traditional Chinese kite and let fly in Tiananmen Square.

Adventure activities

Trekking: along the Great Wall. Try the challenging 4-hour walk along some of the ruins that run from Simatai to Jinshanling.

Skiing: take to the slopes in Yabuli, Heilongjiang Province, in China's far northeast between December and April.

Ballooning: in Yangshuo, Guangxi province. See the spectacular karst scenery from an equally spectacular angle.

Hiking: take a vigorous hike up one of China's many scenic mountains. Popular destinations are Huangshan, Taishan, Emeishan and Wutaishan.

Ice skating: rub elbows with a mass of Chinese skaters moving in every direction around Beijing's Houhai.

Horse-back riding: take to the trails on horseback in the grasslands of Inner Mongolia or Tibet.

Biking: through the colourful Guangxi or Yunnan countryside.

Paragliding: out at the Ming Tombs reservoir or close to Beijing.

Sand-sledding: on the Singing Sand Dunes of Dunhuang, Gansu province.

Canoeing: paddle to Yangshuo on the Li River.

Visit Beijing's hutong

For long-time residents of Beijing, there is probably nothing more emblematic of the city than its idyllic – but quickly disappearing – courtyard houses and winding alleyways, known as *hutong.* These have been around for some seven centuries, dating back to the Yuan Dynasty when Kublai Khan established his capital at Dadu, on the site of present-day Beijing. In fact, the word *hutong* is believed to derive from the Mongolian word *hong tong,* which means water well.

During imperial times, there were no street signs labelling the *hutong,* and so their names were passed on orally, some named

after national heroes, some for their location, and some for the business conducted there, such as Cotton Hutong or Hat Hutong. Other names are descriptive. Little Horn Hutong is named for its shape, as one end is much wider than the other. This is one of the smallest *hutong* in the city, its narrow end just 60cm (23in) wide.

Despite the changes taking place around the city, time seems to stand still here. Vendors sell *baozi,* or steamed meat buns, on the street, next to horse carts piled high with watermelons. Peddlers push carts down the street, shouting to announce their presence. Some chant rhymes to advertise their wares, and others make a particular sound that residents immediately associate with a certain product. Small children crowd around a hawker with dozens of small woven baskets no larger than a plum, inside which are crickets.

There are many fine *hutong* neighbourhoods close to the Forbidden City. The best way to enjoy them is simply to stroll. The lanes just to the west of Qianhai Lake are particularly appealing. Nearby, southeast of Beijing's Drum Tower, is another huge block of *hutong*. Nearly all of the east to west lanes that run between Dianmen Waidajie and Jiandaokou Nandajie are *hutong* of one variety or another. Running north to south through the centre of this block is Nanluogu Xiang (Drum and Gong Alley), well known for its collection of coffee houses and cafés. This is a great spot to while away an afternoon in atmospheric surrounds.

Places to take the children

BEIJING
Beijing Chaoyang Theatre
The China Acrobatic Troupe offers a nightly performance including tightrope walking, plate spinning and mind-boggling gymnastics.

✉ 36 Dongsanhuanbei Lu, Chaoyang District ☎ (010) 6507 2421 🕐 Daily 5:15pm and 7:15pm (show lasts 30 mins, approx) ✋ Expensive

Le Cool
Large ice-skating rink inside Beijing's classiest mall. Prada, Cartier and Louis Vitton provide distraction for the grown ups.

✉ B2, China World Shopping Mall, 1 Jianguomenwai Dajie ☎ (010) 6505 5776; www.lecoolicerink.com 🕐 10–10 ✋ Moderate

HONG KONG
Ocean Park
Including an amusement park and a pair of giant pandas given to mark the 10th anniversary of the 1997 handover of Hong Kong.

✉ Wong Chuk Hang Road, Aberdeen, Hong Kong Island ☎ (852) 2552 0291; www.oceanpark.com.hk 🕐 Daily 10–6 ✋ Expensive

Hong Kong Disneyland
The resort has been modelled on the original 1950s Disneyland theme park in California and has virtually identical attractions.

✉ Lantau Island ☎ (852) 1 830 830; www.hongkongdisneyland.com 🕐 Daily 10am – 8pm (approx) ✋ Expensive

Hong Kong Space Museum
Great interactive displays and a huge Space Theatre planetarium.

✉ 10 Salisbury Road, Tsim Sha Tsui, Kowloom, Hong Kong ☎ (852) 2721 0226; www.lcsd.gov.hk 🕐 Mon, Wed–Fri 1–9, Sat,Sun 10–9 ✋ Inexpensive

SHANGHAI
Science and Technology Museum
Interactive museum split into 12 main themes including Earth

Exploration, Children's Technoland, Light of Wisdom, Spectrum of Life, and Cradle of Designers.

✉ 2000 Shijidadao, Century Park, Pudong ☎ (021) 6862 2000; www.sstm.org.cn 🕓 Tue–Sun 9–5:15 🖐 Moderate

Shanghai Centre Theatre

Home to the Shanghai Acrobatics Troupe who put on a daily hour-and-a-half show featuring breathtaking feats of strength and skill.

✉ 1376 Nanjing Xilu ☎ (021) 6279 8948 🕓 Shows begin at 7:30pm. The venue is sometimes used for music concerts. On these occasions, the acrobatics show is cancelled 🖐 Expensive

Shanghai Zoo

One of China's better zoos. Unusual and rare animals include the South China tiger, Siberian tiger, red goral, ring-tailed lemur and oriental white stork. Other attractions include a roller-skating rink, and children's playground.

✉ 2381 Hongqiao Lu (near the old airport) ☎ (021) 6268 7775 ext 8000; www.shanghaizoo.cn 🕓 Daily 6:30–5 🖐 Inexpensive

Stunning views

Avenue of Stars, Hong Kong: this walkway is the best spot to drink in the spectacular city skyline of Hong Kong Island.

Beihai, Huangshan: the Beihai (North Sea) is best viewed from Huangshan's Refreshing Terrace. Watch in awe as a sea of mist courses through the valley below.

Jinmao Tower, Shanghai: ignore Shanghai's Pearl Tower and head up to the 88th floor observation deck of the Jinmao Tower, behind, to get the best view on the city's famous forest of high-rises.

Lake Karakul, Xinjiang: close to the China-Pakistan border, Lake Karakul is a dreamy vista of teardrop-blue water and snow-dipped mountain peaks. The lake is famed for its hypnotizing hues.

Nanshan Night View, Chonging: take a nighttime cable-car across the Yangtze, make the climb up to Nanshan Park and turn around to see the lights of Chongqing reflected in the river.

Qinghai–Tibet Railway: this remarkable railway journey features a host of spectacular views. Among the best is the look-out from the 5,072m-high (16,636ft) Tanggula Pass, the gateway to Tibet.

Tiananmen Square by night, Beijing: Tiananmen Square takes on a completely different feel at night when the crowds thin out and the buildings are lit with thousands of golden bulbs.

Xingping, Guilin: sailing north on the Li River from Yangshuo, meander past bamboo groves and commorant fisherment before reaching Xingping and the famous sugarloaf-shaped mountains.

Yongjiajie, Zhangjiajie: this cliff-side walkway includes a iron bridge, through which you can peer 300m (984ft) down to the ground, and a sweeping vista of knarled quartzite stone columns.

Exploring

China has a rich history, unique culture and an astonishing level of geographic diversity, but it's the sheer energy of the country that grips you. This is a land where high-rises sprout as quickly as green vegetables, and it's breathtaking to behold.

In a country of 1.3 billion people, China's ceaseless hustle and bustle is one of its great marvels. Step out into the city at night and your senses will be assailed: smells from whirring extractor fans, music from shops that never seem to close, bright lights from overhanging street signs.

Meanwhile China's rural residents carry on serenely. From the lonely Inner Mongolian grasslands in the north, to the lush Yunnanese jungles in the south; the majestic snow peaks of Tibet out west to the rice paddies of the eastern plains, the Chinese countryside reveals a quite different face of this remarkable country.

Beijing and Northern China

Beijing is where the idealized 'costume-drama' China of the movies meets the dynamic 'boom-town' China written about in today's newspapers. The city has the densest concentration of historic buildings and traditional attractions and yet has become synonymous with daring architectural designs and radical modern art.

Beijing

The city's climate is similarly polarized: scorching, sweaty summers versus freezing, dry winters. Unusually for a capital, Beijing lies on flat terrain close to neither river nor sea. Unconstrained by natural obstructions, the city has grown into a sprawling, bustling metropolis.

Northeast of Beijing is the land best known in the west as

Manchuria. Its importance as an industrial heartland explains the many attempts by China's neighbours to wrest the area from its grasp. Indeed, the Russian, Korean and Japanese influences evident today give the region its unique character. Inner Mongolia, meanwhile, is famed for its stunning desert and grassland scenery.

BEIJING

It was not until Kublai Khan established the Yuan Dynasty in the 13th century that Beijing, then called Dadu, or Great Capital, became the capital of all of China for the first time. In 1368, the Chinese changed the name to Beiping, or 'northern peace'. In the Ming Dynasty, Emperor Yongle, known as the architect of Beijing, began a massive rebuilding of the city, including the Temple of Heaven and the Imperial Palace, a project that took 14 years to complete. To protect the city, a massive wall, complete with looming watchtowers, was erected. After the Manchus overthrew the Ming Dynasty in 1644, they expanded the Forbidden City and built several pleasure palaces on the outskirts.

Beijing remained the imperial capital under the Qing, though the Nationalists set up their capital in Nanjing in the 1920s and moved to Chongqing during the war with Japan (1937–1945). Beijing was

restored to top spot in 1949 when the Red Army claimed victory in the civil war against the Nationalists. The city changed dramatically over the subsequent five decades, with the old city wall being torn down in the 1950s.

The city's real boom came after economic reforms were launched in the 1980s though things have gone into overdrive since Beijing successfully bid to host the 2008 Olympics. Improved infrastructure, better public transport and literally thousands of gleaming new buildings have been the result. Unfortunately, many old lanes or *hutong,* courtyard houses and historical sites have disappeared under the weight of the wrecking ball as new apartment complexes and office buildings rise in their place. The authorities today face the challenge of promoting modernization without erasing the charm of the old city.

✚ 4D

Baiyunguan (White Cloud Temple)

This is one of the major Taoist temples in China, and the head quarters of the China Taoist Association. The first Taoist monastery was erected here in the 8th century, but the present structure underwent major renovations in 1956 and 1981. The monastery conducts traditional ceremonies and is regularly crowded with followers and tourists on holy days. Temple decorations contain many religious symbols, including Lingzhi fungus and storks.

✚ *Beijing 2d* ✉ 6 Baiyunguan Jie, Xibianmenwai, Xuanwu District ☎ (010) 6346 3531 🕐 Daily 8:30–4 💷 Inexpensive 🚇 Nanlishilu 🚌 46, 48, 114, 308

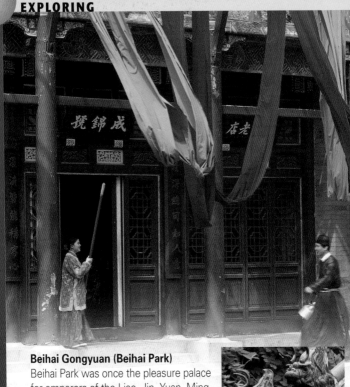

Beihai Gongyuan (Beihai Park)

Beihai Park was once the pleasure palace for emperors of the Liao, Jin, Yuan, Ming and Qing dynasties.

The most important structure here is the Hall of Receiving Light, which is home to a 5m-high (16ft) white jade Buddha said to have been a gift from Burma to the Empress Dowager Cixi. This is where emperors rested when on their way to the western suburbs.

Qionghua Island, in Lake Beihai, is the location of the White Dagoba and the Pavilion of Benevolent Voice, from where there are excellent views of the surrounding lakes.

✚ *Beijing 5b* ✉ Wenjin Jie, Xicheng District ☎ (010) 6403 1102
🕐 Nov–May daily 6:30pm–8pm; Jun–Oct daily 6am–10pm 🎟 Inexpensive
🚌 5, 101, 103, 109. To south gate: 13, 42, 105, 107, 111, 118

Fayuansi (Fayuan Temple)

This temple was built in 654 in the Tang Dynasty to honour soldiers who were killed in battle. Home of the Buddhist Theoretical Institute, the temple is often crowded with Buddhist monks going to and from classes. The temple houses an excellent collection of old artefacts and manuscripts dating from the Ming and Qing dynasties.

➕ *Beijing 3f* ✉ 7 Fayuansiqian Jie, Xuanwu District
☎ (010) 6353 4171 🕔 Thu–Tue 8:30–11, 2–4
✋ Inexpensive 🚇 Xuanwumen
🚌 6, 10, 50, 53, 56, 61, 109

Gugong (Forbidden City)

Best places to see, ➤ 42–43

Guguang Xiangtai (Observatory)

The Chinese have placed great importance on astronomy since ancient times, with dynasties building observatories in their capitals so that astronomers could produce the official calendar that regulated the agricultural year and sacred ceremonies. Kublai Khan established an observatory just north of here during the Yuan Dynasty. The Ming court built the present observatory at this watchtower in 1442, and it remained in use until 1929. The original Ming and Qing instruments are displayed outside on the second level terrace.

➕ *Beijing 8d* ✉ 2 Dongbiaobei Hutong, Chaoyang District ☎ (010) 6524 2202
🕔 Tue–Sun 9–11:30, 1–4 ✋ Inexpensive
🚇 Jianguomen 🚌 1, 4, 8, 9, 20, 43, 44, 57

Jingshan Gongyuan (Prospect Hill Park)

Jingshan Park, which dates back to the Yuan Dynasty, was once the private playground of the imperial family. When the moat was dug for the Forbidden City, the excavated earth was used to create five hills north of the Imperial Palace. The Ten Thousand Spring Pavilion at the top of the central peak provides a stunning panoramic view of the gold and russet roofscape of the Forbidden City and Beihai Park.

✚ *Beijing 5b* ✉ Jingshan Park, north of the Forbidden City
☎ (010) 6404 4071 ⏰ Summer daily 6–8:30, winter daily 7–8
✋ Inexpensive 🚌 5, 101, 103, 111

Kong Miao (Confucius Temple)

Confucius is considered the most important thinker in Chinese history, and his teachings were taken as the orthodox school of thought from the Han to the Qing Dynasty. First built in 1287, the temple underwent a major renovation in 1784. The quiet courtyard is lined by cypress and pine trees, and on the two sides of the yard is a collection of 188 stelae, bearing the names and birthplaces of the successful candidates in the imperial service exams from 1416–1904.

🚩 *Beijing 7a* ✉ 13 Guozijian Jie, Dongcheng District ☎ (010) 8401 1977
🕐 8:30–5 💲 Inexpensive
🚇 Yonghegong
🚌 2, 13, 18, 44, 104, 108, 116

Mao Zhuxi Jiniantang (Mausoleum of Mao Zedong)

After Chairman Mao Zedong died in 1976, the party ignored his wish to be cremated and ordered that his body be embalmed. Within one year, the mausoleum was built at the southern end of Tiananmen Square, and his body was placed in a crystal coffin draped with the red flag of the Communist Party. The coffin, located in the Hall of Mourning, is raised from its underground refrigeration unit each morning. A visit here takes just a few minutes as viewers are not permitted to stop.

🚩 *Beijing 5d* ✉ Tiananmen Square ☎ (010) 6513 2277
🕐 Mon–Sat 8:30–11:30, Mon, Wed, Fri 2–4 💲 Inexpensive
🚇 Tiananmen, Qianmen 🚌 1, 2, 4, 5, 9, 10, 17, 22, 44, 47, 48, 53, 59, 110, 116

Niujie Libaisi (Ox Street Mosque)

One of the oldest mosques in Beijing, it was built by the son of an Arab imam who came to China in 996, but it has since undergone numerous renovations. Many of the early Muslims who arrived in China during the Yuan Dynasty are buried on the grounds. The original structure was built in an Islamic style; the present building has a distinctive Chinese facade. Immediately inside the gate is a hexagonal building called the Moon Watching Tower. In front of this is a memorial archway, and then the main prayer hall facing Mecca in the west. In the centre is a minaret from which the faithful are called to prayer five times a day.

✚ *Beijing 3f* ✉ 88 Niu Jie, Xuanwu District ☎ (010) 6353 2564 🕔 Daily 7–7 ✋ Inexpensive 🚌 61

Qianmen

Entry to the Forbidden City was controlled by a series of nine gates. Qianmen was the main point of transit between the northern Tartar district and the southern Chinese district of Beijing.

The gate was built during the 15th century. The Jianlou is just south of Qianmen, and the two gates were originally joined. At every winter solstice the emperor passed through this gate to pray at the Temple of Heaven. Qianmen Dajie, running south of the gate, is being given a major make-over for the 2008 Olympics and is expected to be a pedestrian street with shops and restaurants in traditional Qing-era buildings.

✚ *Beijing 5e* ✉ South side of Mao Memorial Hall ☎ (010) 6522 9386 🕔 Tue–Sun 8:30–4 ✋ Inexpensive 🚇 Qianmen 🚌 1, 2, 4, 5, 9, 10, 17, 22, 44, 47, 48, 53, 59, 110, 116

Shishan Ling (Ming Tombs)

Thirteen of the 16 Ming emperors are buried at the Ming Tombs, along with their wives. However, only three of those tombs are open to members of the public. Changling, the burial site of the third Ming emperor, Yongle, is considered the most important. It is said that 16 concubines were buried alive with the emperor, a practice that was abandoned later in the Ming Dynasty. Dingling, the tomb of Emperor Wanli, took six years to complete, and Wanli gave a party in his own funeral chamber to mark its completion. The coffins of the emperor and his two empresses and more than 3,000 artefacts are on display in the tomb and two small museums. The Ming tombs are approached by the Sacred Way, an impressive avenue leading to the tombs which is lined with an honour guard of 12 pairs of statues, each carved from a single stone.

➕ 4D ✉ Changping County, Tianshoushannan Lu ☎ (010) 6076 1888
🕐 Apr–Oct daily 8–5:30; Nov–Mar daily 8:30–5 ✋ Moderate
🚌 Direct bus from Qianmen or Beijing Railway Station

Si Baita (Temple Of The White Dagoba)

This 50m-tall (164ft) dagoba (pagoda), in the Miaoying Monastery, was built in 1079 during the Liao Dynasty, and was significantly expanded and redecorated by Kublai Khan during the Yuan Dynasty. The dagoba's brilliance is said to be due to the fact that it is painted with an expensive whitewash containing a large amount of pulverised seashells. The temple was rebuilt in the Ming Dynasty, and was once again restored following damage during the Cultural Revolution and an earthquake in 1976.

➕ *Beijing 5b* ✉ 171 Fuchengmennei Dajie, Xicheng District ☎ (010) 6616 0211 🕐 Daily 8:30–5 ✋ Inexpensive 🚌 7, 13, 38, 42, 101, 102, 103

Soong Qingling Guju (Former Residence of Soong Qingling)

Soong Qingling (1893–1981) was one of the most prominent women of modern China. Educated at Wesleyan College in Georgia, USA, she later married Nationalist leader Sun Yatsen. The residence has a large garden with ponds, cypress trees and pavilions. The house has photos and Soong's personal effects; the bedroom and study remain as they were when Soong lived here.

✚ *Beijing 5a* ✉ 46 Houhaibeiyan, Xicheng District ☎ (010) 6404 4205; (010) 6403 5858 🕔 Apr–Oct daily 9–5:30; Nov–Mar daily 9–4:30 💷 Inexpensive 🚌 5

Tiananmen Guangchang (Tiananmen Square)

Tiananmen Square is one of the largest public squares in the world, covering 100ha (247 acres). A public gathering place during the Ming and Qing dynasties, buildings stood on the two sides of a central path leading to the entrance of the Forbidden City. The square is the political heart of modern China. Beijing university students came here to protest Japanese demands on China in 1919, and it was from the rostrum of the Gate of Heavenly Peace that Chairman Mao announced the establishment of the People's Republic of China in 1949. Red Guards held huge rallies in the square during the Cultural Revolution (1966–1976), and a million people gathered here in 1976 to mourn the passing of Communist leader Zhou Enlai. In 1989, the square was the site of massive anti-government student demonstrations. Just behind the monument is the Mausoleum of Mao Zedong (➤ 79) and Qianmen (➤ 80). On the west side of the square is the Great Hall of the People, where China's parliament, the National People's Congress, meets. The National Museum of China, the building on the east side, is undergoing renovation and is expected to remain closed until 2010.

➕ *Beijing 5d* ✉ Centre of Beijing City 🚇 Tiananmen Xi, Tiananmen Dong, Qianmen 🚌 2, 4, 5, 9, 10, 17, 22, 44, 47, 48, 53, 59, 110, 116

Tiantan (Temple Of Heaven)

The Temple of Heaven is one of the best examples of religious architecture in China. Construction began in 1406 during the reign of Yongle and took 14 years to complete. The complex contains three main buildings where the emperor went during the winter solstice to offer prayers and sacrifices for a good harvest. The emperor spent the night preceding the ceremony fasting in the Hall of Abstinence. The Hall of Prayer for Good Harvests stands 39m (128ft) tall and is supported by 28 wooden pillars topped by three conical roofs. The last person to use the hall was president Yuan Shikai, of the newly established republic, who had imperial ambitions and who offered imperial sacrifices on the winter solstice in 1914. The Hall of the Imperial Vault of Heaven, located in the centre, stored the ceremonial tablets used in rituals. Echo Wall, a circular brick wall surrounding the Imperial Vault, has the acoustical ability to enable two people standing at opposite points to hear each other whisper. The circular mound of the Altar of Heaven, to the south, is where the emperor offered sacrifices and prayed.

✚ *Beijing 6f* ✉ Tiantandong Lu, Chongwen District
☎ (010) 6702 8866 ⏰ Park: daily 6–9. Temple buildings: Apr–Oct daily 8–6; Nov–Mar daily 8–5 (last ticket sold 90 minutes before closing)
✋ Moderate 🚌 2, 15, 16, 17, 20, 35, 36, 106, 110, 116

Wuta Si (Five Pagoda Temple)

This Indian-style temple was built in the 15th century during the reign of Yongle. The temple has five pagodas, each decorated with detailed Buddhist bas-reliefs. The temple was looted by Anglo-French troops following the Second Opium War in 1860 and by Western soldiers during the Boxer Rebellion in 1900.

✚ *Beijing 1a* ✉ 24 Wutasicun, Haidian ☎ (010) 6217 3836 ⏰ Tue–Sun 9–4 ✋ Inexpensive (free Wed) 🚇 Xizhimen 🚌 4, 5, 105, 107, 111, 114

Xuanwumen Tang (Southern Cathedral)

The Southern Cathedral, also known as the Cathedral of the Immaculate Conception, is the oldest Catholic church in Beijing. It was first erected in the middle of the 16th century by Matteo Ricci, an Italian Jesuit missionary who arrived in China in 1583 and received permission to live in Beijing in 1601 after impressing Emperor Wanli with his knowledge of maths and science. The cathedral was rebuilt in 1657, and a stone tablet erected at the time still stands in the yard, inscribed with the words 'Cathedral Built on Imperial Order'. The present structure dates back to 1904.

✚ *Beijing 4d* ✉ 141 Qianmenxi Dajie, Xuanwu District ☎ (010) 6603 7139 ⏱ Services in Latin, Mon–Sat 6:30am, Sun 6:30, 7:30 and 8:30am. Service in English, Sun 10am, 4pm 🚇 Xuanwumen 🚌 5, 15, 25, 44, 45, 48, 49

Xu Beihong Bowuguan (Xu Beihong Museum)

One of the most famous modern Chinese painters, Xu Beihong (1895–1953) is especially known for his vivid paintings of galloping horses. The museum has seven rooms, five dedicated to displaying Xu's sketches and paintings and offering an introduction to his life and work. His painting studio and sitting room are displayed here, with his brushes and paints on a table as if ready for use. An unfinished oil painting stands on an easel, as it did when he died. The museum also includes 1,200 paintings by other famous Chinese painters, 10,000 rare books, illustrations and stone rubbings.

✚ Beijing 4a ✉ 53 Xinjiekoubei Dajie, Xicheng District ☎ (010) 6225 2265 🕐 Tue–Sun 9–4:30 💷 Inexpensive 🚇 Jishuitan 🚌 22, 27, 38, 44, 47

Yiheyuan (Summer Palace)

This complex of buildings and gardens dates back 800 years when the first emperor of the Jin Dynasty built the Gold Mountain Palace at the site now known as Longevity Hill. Succeeding dynasties expanded the complex. The imperial court would come here in the summer to get away from the heat of Beijing. The palace was damaged by Anglo-French troops in 1860 during the Second Opium War, and was burned down by Western soldiers in retaliation for the Boxer Rebellion in 1900, but it was restored in 1903. The 700m (763yds) Long Corridor, a long covered wooden walkway that runs across the south shore of the lake, is decorated with auspicious symbols and landscape paintings on the beams. Emperor Guangxu and Empress Dowager Cixi received ministers in the Hall of Benevolent

Longevity. The Hall of Jade Ripples is where Cixi put Guangxu under house arrest in 1898 after the young emperor attempted to carry out far-reaching reforms. He remained here until his death in 1908, allegedly poisoned by Cixi, who died one day later. At the west end of the lake is the famous marble boat built by Cixi with money intended for creating a modern Chinese navy.

✚ *Beijing 1a (off map)* ✉ Yiheyuan, northwest of Haidian District ☎ (010) 6288 1144
🕐 Apr–Oct daily 6:30–6; Nov–Mar daily 7–5
💰 Moderate 🚌 301, 303, 304, 332, 333, 346, 726, 801, 808, 904

Yonghe Gong (Lama Temple)

After Qing Emperor Yongzheng ascended the throne in 1723, his former palace, built in 1694, was converted into a Lamaist temple. Lamaism, the popular name for Tibetan Buddhism, was practiced by the Manchu rulers during the Qing Dynasty. During the reign of Qianlong the temple became a centre of learning for the Yellow Hat sect of Tibetan Buddhism, and exercised considerable religious and political influence. At its peak, some 1,500 Tibetan, Mongol and Chinese Lamas lived here. The temple was shut down during the Cultural Revolution, but was saved from destruction by Zhou Enlai. The temple is a complex of five halls and courtyards.

✚ Beijing 7a ✉ 12 Yonghegong Dajie, Dongcheng District (near the northeast corner of Second Ring Road)
☎ (010) 6404 34499 🕔 Apr–Oct daily 9–4:30; Nov–Mar daily 9–4 ✋ Inexpensive 🚇 Yonghegong 🚌 13, 44, 106, 107, 116

Yuanmingyuan (Old Summer Palace)

This palace, a complex of three large gardens, was built for the emperor Qianlong during the Qing Dynasty. It was seriously damaged by Anglo-French troops in 1860 after the Second Opium War, and again during the Boxer Rebellion in 1900. Little is left of it today except for some broken pillars and masonry lying scattered around, though the gardens are very pleasant. The Garden History Exhibition Hall has drawings and models of the palace during better days.

➕ *Beijing 1a (off map)* ✉ 28 Qinghua Lu, Haidian District
☎ (010) 6262 8501 🕓 Apr–Oct daily 7–7; Nov–Mar 7–5:30
✋ Inexpensive 🚌 331, 365, 375

Zhong Lou and Gu Lou (Bell and Drum Tower)

The Drum Tower was built in 1424 during the Ming Dynasty. During imperial times, 24 drums would announce the night watches. The Bell Tower was erected in 1747. The massive bronze bell was rung every evening until 1924, when the last emperor was forced to leave the Forbidden City. It is said the bell could be heard for a distance of over 20km (12.5 miles).

➕ *Beijing 5a* ✉ 9 Zhonggulou Daijie/Dianmenwai Dajie, Dongcheng District
☎ (010) 6401 2674 🕓 Daily 9–5 ✋ Inexpensive 🚌 5, 58, 60, 107

Zhoukoudian

In 1929 the discovery of the first skull of Peking Man was found at this site on Dragon Bone Hill, dating back 300,000–500,000 years. The museum at Zhoukoudian introduces the Zhoukoudian culture, including displays of implements used by Peking Man. The fossils vanished during World War II and have never been recovered.

➕ *Beijing 1e (off map)*
✉ Nanfangshan, Zhoukoudian Village, Jingxi, 48km (30 miles) southwest of Beijing

a cycling tour

around Beijing

Begin at Donghuamen, the east gate of the Forbidden City. Turn left at the gate and follow the red wall of the Forbidden City, stopping along the way to listen to amateur Peking opera singers and musicians.

Ride to the front courtyard of the Forbidden City, cross the courtyard, and exit on the opposite side. Continue along the wall until you come to Nanchang Jie, the west side of the palace. Turn right and ride north to the corner and then turn right at Jingshanqian Jie, and ride past Jingshan Gongyuan (Prospect Hill) on your left. Ride around the park by turning left at the next corner, left again and then right onto Dianmennei Dajie. Turn left at Dianmenxi Dajie and, having passed Qianhai, or Front Lake, take the first road on your right.

On this peaceful street you'll find Chinese sitting beneath willow trees playing Chinese chess or doing exercises.

Cross the tiny Silver Ingot Bridge that spans a channel in the lake and turn left along Houhaibeiyan, which runs along the east side of Houhai, or the Rear Lake. From here continue on to the junction with Deshengmennei Dajie. Turn left and cross over the bridge. You'll soon come to the Kong Yiji Restaurant (see listings) inside a circular whitewashed Chinese Gate.

The restaurant is named after Lu Xun's short story of the same name.

After lunch jump back on your bicycle, turn left into the Yangfang Hutong and peddle

to Liuyin Jie, on your right. Head down this street to Gongwangfu, the former palace of Prince Gong, younger brother of the Xianfeng Emperor (1851–1861).

Distance: 3.5km (2 miles)
Time: 2–3 hours
Start point: Donghuamen, East Gate, Forbidden City ✚ *Beijing 6c*
End point: Gongwangfu (Prince Gong's Mansion) ✚ *Beijing 5a*
Lunch: Kong Yiji Restaurant
(➤ 103)
✉ Deshengmennei Dajie
☎ (010) 6618 4917

Heibi Province

CHANGCHENG (THE GREAT WALL)

Best places to see, ➤ 38–39.

CHENGDE

In 1703, Emperor Kangxi began the construction of a **Summer Palace** in Chengde, known in Chinese as the 'Mountain Retreat to Escape the Heat'. The palace was used by Qing emperors while on hunting trips or making military inspection tours. The palace area served as the administrative and residential quarters of the emperors. The Hall of Frugality and Calm, which is built of cedar wood, is where the emperor met with court officials, generals, foreign envoys and the heads of northern tribes. The Hall of Refreshing Mists and Waves was the royal bedroom, but also was the site of famous historical events, such as the signing of the so-called unequal treaties with the Europeans in the 19th century.

Twelve temples were built outside the palace walls, eight of them belonging to the Yellow Sect of Buddhism for the purpose of winning the support of Mongolians and Tibetans. The Putuozongcheng Temple, the largest and most interesting of the eight, resembles the Potala Palace in Lhasa. The Temple of Sumeru, Happiness and Longevity is a replica of the Tashilhunpo in Shigatse, and has a roof with 'fish-scale' ridges and marvellous dragons. The Puning Temple is a synthesis of Han and Tibetan architectural styles.

✚ 4C ✉ 256km (159 miles) northeast of Beijing 🍴 Restaurants along Shanxiying Jie ($) 🚌 Daily from Beijing and Tianjin 🚆 Express train N211 from Beijing Station or the 2101/2105/2108 service from Beijing North Station

Imperial Summer Palace

✉ Lizhengmen Dajie 🕐 16 Apr– 14 Oct daily 7–5:30; 15 Oct–15 Apr daily 7–4:30 ✋ Moderate

QING DONG LING (EASTERN QING TOMBS)

Five emperors, 14 empresses and 136 concubines are buried at the Eastern Qing Tombs, including Kangxi, Qianlong, Xuanfeng, Tongzhi and Empress Dowager Cixi. Emperor Shunzhi chose the site because of its good fengshui, or geomancy. The marble vault of Qianlong is the most interesting, with beautifully carved Buddhas. Cixi's tomb is also decorated with imperial motifs such as dragons and phoenixes.

✚ 4D ✉ Just before Changrui, Zunhua County, Hebei Province, 125km (77.5 miles) east of Beijing

QING XI LING (WESTERN QING TOMBS)

The Western Qing Tombs house the remains of four Qing emperors: Yongzheng, Jiaqing, Daoguang and Guangxu along with a number of empresses, princes and concubines. The main tomb is that of Yongzheng, the first Qing emperor to be buried here.

✚ 3D ✉ At the foot of Yongning Mountain, Yi County, Hebei Province, 140km (87 miles) southwest of Beijing

Heilongjiang Province

HARBIN

Harbin, literally 'where the fishing nets dry', dates back to 1097, when it was first settled by ancestors of the Manchu people. It remained a small hunting and fishing village until 1896, when the Russian czar and the Qing court agreed that Russia would build a railroad linking Dalian, Harbin, and the Trans-Siberian Railroad with Vladivostok. Today, the capital of Heilongjiang Province, the city retains many traces of its Russian heritage.

Russian Orthodox churches were seriously damaged during the Cultural Revolution, but some have been renovated. **St Sofia's Church** is a good example of Byzantine architecture. The church, completed in 1932, is now the Municipal Architecture and Art Museum, which houses an excellent exhibition of the architectural history of the city. The main part of the church is laid out in the shape of a crucifix, with the main hall capped by a large green tipped roof.

✚ 6A ✉ Capital of Heilongjiang Province, northeast China
🚉 Daily from Beijing ✈ Harbin Airport
❓ Ice Lantern Festival, 5 Jan–15 Feb

St Sofia's Church

✉ 88 Toulong Jie, between Zhaolin Jie and Diduan Jie ⏰ Daily 9:30–5 💰 Inexpensive 🚌 13, 16, 23,101, 102, 103, 116

Shaanxi Province

XI'AN

Formerly Chang'an, Xi'an served as the capital of China for 1,100 years, and the treasure trove of artefacts – notably the world-famous Terracotta Warriors – are a reminder of the city's glorious past. Xi'an reached the height of its glory during the Tang Dynasty when it represented the eastern terminus of the Silk Road. It was

arguably the greatest city in the world during this era, famous for its beautiful temples, grand mosques and magnificent palaces.

Down the road from the Terracotta site is Huaqing Hot Springs, used as an Imperial resort for hundreds of years. The palace includes gardens and elaborate structures dating back to the Qing Dynasty. It is also famous as the place where Generalissimo Chiang Kaishek was kidnapped in 1936. Other popular sites are the Ming Dynasty city wall, the Grand Mosque, the Bell Tower, where a bronze bell struck each morning as the city gates opened, and the Drum Tower, which sounded the evening curfew.

🚩 1F ✉ Capital of Shaanxi Province 🚌 Buses to Luoyang 🚆 Daily from Beijing, Chengdu, Guangzhou, Shanghai ✈ Xiguan International Airport (40km/25 miles northwest of city) 🛈 Xian Railway Station ☎ (029) 8745 3872

Cheng Qiang (City Walls)

Xian's city wall is regarded as the most complete of its kind in China. Recent restoration means it's now possible to walk or cycle the entire 13.7km (8.5 miles) circumference. The 12m-high (39ft) wall was built in 1374 but was raised on the foundations of a much older structure – the Imperial compound of the Tang emperors. You can scale the wall at the four compass points though most visitors chose the South Gate where you can hire a bicycle.

🕐 Apr–Oct daily 7:30–9:30; Nov–Mar daily 8–6 ✋ Moderate (the wall-top tram charges 5RMB per stop or 50RMB for the entire circuit)

Da Yan Ta (Greater Wild Goose Pagoda)

Regarded by many as the symbol of the city, the Big Goose Pagoda is located in the Da Ci'en Si (Temple of Maternal Grace) and is the oldest building in Xian. The seven-storey structure was built in AD652 at the behest of legendary monk, Xuanzang, who walked his way to India in the name of Buddhist learning. About 2km (1.6 miles) northwest is Jianfu Si (Jianfu Temple) which houses the Little Goose Pagoda. At 43m (141ft), it's smaller but, being closer to the old city, the views from the top are excellent.

Da Yan Ta

✉ Yanta Lu ☎ (029) 8521 5014 🕐 Daily 8–6:30 ✋ Inexpensive 🚌 610 (separate tickets to enter temple and climb pagoda)

Xiaoyan Ta

✉ Youyi Xilu ☎ (029) 8781 1081 🕐 8:30–4:30 ✋ Inexpensive 🚌 610

Shaanxi History Museum (Shanxi Lishi Bowuguan)

The Shaanxi History Museum is second only to the Shanghai Museum in showcasing the best of Chinese history. Opened in 1991 in a huge Tang-style building, the museum has a collection of around 370,000 items. There are particularly impressive displays from Xian's – and China's – two greatest eras, the Han and Tang dynasties, as well as four original Terracotta Warrior statues taken from close to the tomb of Qin Shi Huang.

✉ 91 Xiaozhai Donglu ☎ (029) 8521 9422; www.sxhm.com 🕐 16 Mar–14 Nov daily 8:30–6:30; 15 Nov–15 Mar 9–5:30 🍴 Moderate 🚌 5, 14, 610, 701

The Old City

A cluster of important landmarks lies in the heart of old Xian. The Daqingzhen Si (Great Mosque, 8–8:30; inexpensive) offers the best sense of the city's cosmopolitan history. Originally built in AD743 by Persian merchants, it was moved to Huajue Xiang in the 14th century, though the current building dates only to the 18th century. With a traditional Chinese pagoda serving as the minaret, the mosque melds a traditional Chinese temple layout with Persian embellishments. Close by are Zhong Lou and Gu Lou (Bell and Drum Towers, Nov–Mar 8:30–5:30; Apr–Oct 8:30–9:30, inexpensive) facing each other across Bell Drum Tower Square. In Xian's past glory days, the bell would have been rung as the city gates opened at dawn, and the drum struck as they were closed at dusk.

BINGMAYONG (TERRACOTTA WARRIORS)

Best places to see, ➤ 136–37.

Shanxi Province

DATONG XUANKONG SI (HANGING TEMPLE)

The Hanging Temple has been clinging precariously to the near vertical cliff of Golden Dragon Gorge for some 14 centuries. Constructed by Taoist monks known as 'Feathered Scholars', and renovated numerous times, the six main halls and other rooms are linked by a mixture of winding corridors, bridges and boardwalks. Known in Chinese as the 'Monastery in Mid-Air', the temple was built in stages on pillars positioned in both natural and man-made holes found in the face of the cliff.

➕ 3D ✉ 75km (46.5 miles) southeast of Datong, Shanxi Province
☎ (0352) 832 7795 🕐 Daily 8–6 ✋ Moderate 🚌 Bus from Datong to
Hunyuan. Minibuses from Hunyuan

PINGYAO

Pingyao, Shanxi Province, was settled some 2,700 years ago
as a military base, surrounded by walls made of rammed earth.
The city was enlarged, and the walls rebuilt in 1370. Pingyao
remains one of the best-preserved ancient walled cities in China.
In several locations there are urn-shaped enclosures which were
designed to trap invaders. There are 3,000 crenels and 72 small
watchtowers, symbolizing the 72 main disciples and 3,000
students of Confucius, with taller watchtowers at the four corners.
➕ 2E ✉ 100km (62 miles) south of Taiyuan, Shanxi Province
🍴 Local restaurants near the Tianyuankui Hotel ($) 🚌 Daily from Taiyuan
🚆 Overnight from Beijing, daily from Taiyuan

WUTAISHAN

Wutaishan, or Five Terrace Mountain, is one of China's four sacred
Buddhist mountains. Close to Inner Mongolia, Wutaishan was a
popular pilgrimage site for Mongolians devoted to Tibetan
Buddhism. The Tang and Ming Dynasties were the most
prosperous periods in Wutaishan, when the mountain had no less
than 200 monasteries, but just two remain today – the Nanshan
and the Foguang Monastery, the latter a good example of
traditional Tang Dynasty temple architecture. The valley between
these five peaks centres on the tiny village of Taihuai, which has
dozens of temples dedicated to the Yellow Hat sect of Buddhism.
Taihuai is the jumping off point for travellers.
➕ 3D ✉ Yangboyu Village, Taihuai Town, 240km (149 miles) northeast of
Taiyuan, Shanxi Province ☎ (0350) 654 3133; www.wutaishan.cn
✋ Moderate 🚌 Minibuses from Datong
and Taiyaun. Private minibuses make trips to various temples around
Wutaishan 🚆 Train to Datong or Taiyuan

HOTELS

BEIJING

Bamboo Garden Courtyard (Zhuyuan Binguan) ($$)

Attractive mid-range courtyard hotel to the northwest of the Drum and Bell Towers.

✉ 24 Xiaoshiqiao Hutong, Dongcheng District ☎ (010) 5852 0088; www.bbgh.com.cn

Beijing Raffles Hotel ($$$)

Beijing's oldest hotel was recently refurbished and remains one of its best. A great location within walking distance of Tiananmen Square and the Forbidden City.

✉ 33 Dongchang'an Jie, Dongcheng District ☎ (010) 6513 7766; www.beijing.raffles.com

Beijing Far East International Youth Hostel ($)

Great-value accommodation in a fine location in the middle of Beijing's *hutongs*. Also offers bicycle rental.

✉ 90 Tieshuxie Jie, Qianmenwai ☎ (010) 51958811 ext 3118; www.fareastyh.com

Lusongyuan Binguan ($$)

A traditional walled courtyard hotel in Beijing's historic *hutong* area, originally built by a Mongolian general in the Qing Dynasty.

✉ 22 Banchang Hutong, Kuan Jie, Dongcheng District ☎ (010) 6401 1116

Red Capital Residence ($$$)

A small boutique hotel located in a traditional courtyard house. Each of the five suites has an intriguing name such as 'The Chairman's Residence' or 'Concubine of the East'. The hotel is unmarked. Look for the red door with the number 9.

✉ 9 Dongsi Liutiao, Dongcheng District ☎ (010) 6402 7150; www.redcapitalclub.com.cn

Shangri-La Hotel ($$$)

Another one of China's superb string of Shangri-La hotels. Located in northwest Beijing this place has every conceivable facility, including its own delicatessen and shopping arcade. Well placed for the Summer Palace.

✉ 29 Zizhuyuan Lu, Haidian District ☎ (010) 6841 8002; www.shangri-la.com

St. Regis Hotel ($$$)

A first-class hotel located on the grounds of the historic Beijing International Club and close to Beijing's Jianguomenwai business district. Facilities include a spa and indoor heated pool.

✉ 21 Jianguomenwai Dajie, Chaoyang District ☎ (010) 6460 6688; www.stregis.com

CHENGDE
Mountain Villa Hotel ($)

Perfectly located for the Imperial Summer Palace. The hotel has six restaurants, a business centre and a variety of suites and rooms to suit all tastes.

✉ 127 Xiaonanmen ☎ (0314) 202 5588; www.hemvhotel.com

DATONG
Datong Binguan ($$)

This stately looking hotel is Datong's finest, with modern amenities and comfortable rooms.

✉ 37 Yingbin Xilu ☎ (0352) 586 8666; www.datonghotel.com

HARBIN
Holiday Inn ($–$$)

Close to Harbin's historic Daoliqu area and St Sophia's Church. Facilities include a gym, sauna and massage rooms.

✉ 90 Jingwei Jie ☎ (0451) 8422 6666; e-mail: holiday@public.hr.hl.cn

PINGYAO
Tianyuankui Minfeng Binguan ($)

Fabulously atmospheric Qing-era hotel which used to house travelling merchants. The helpful and friendly staff make booking tickets very easy.

✉ 73 Nan Dajie ☎ (0354) 568 0069; www.pytyk.com

WUTAISHAN
Qixiange Binguan ($$)
The best accommodation at the foot of the mountain. In a peaceful setting close to nature.

✉ 2.5km (1.5 miles) south of Taihuai, near Nanshan Monastery ☎ (0350) 654 2400

Wufeng Binguan ($)
This four-star hotel, located beside the Longquan Temple within the scenic area, is the best hotel in Wutaishan and is well priced.

✉ Taihuai Town ☎ (0350) 644 8988; www.5f-hotel.com

XI'AN
Hyatt Regency Xi'an (Xian Kaiyue Fandian) ($$$)
Situated within the walls of the old city. The grand interior and the high standards of service make this hotel a delight.

✉ 158 Dong Dajie ☎ (029) 8769 1234; www.xian.regency.hyatt.com

RESTAURANTS

BEIJING
Donglaishun ($$)
Muslim-style hot pot. Cook meat and vegetables in a boiling broth at your own table, and then dunk the food into a special sauce.

✉ 5th Floor, Xindong'an Plaza, Wangfujing Dajie ☎ (010) 6528 0932
🕐 Lunch, dinner

Fangshan Restaurant ($$$)
This restaurant serves imperial dishes favoured by the old Manchu rulers. In a lakeside setting inside the east gate of Beihai Park.

✉ 1 Wenjin Jie, inside the east gate of Beihai Park ☎ (010) 6401 1889
🕐 Lunch, dinner

King Roast Duck Restaurant ($$)
Here you can enjoy traditional Peking roast duck cooked in fruit-wood heated ovens.

✉ 24 Jianguomenwai Dajie, Chaoyang District, Beijing ☎ (010) 6515 6908
🕐 Lunch, dinner

Kong Yiji ($$)

Tastefully designed restaurant, located beside Houhai lake and specializing in Zhejiang cuisine. Try *huixiangdou* (lima beans) or *choudoufu* (smelly bean curd), washed down with Shaoxing wine.

✉ 2 Dongming Hutong, Houhai South Bank, Deshengmennei Dajie, Xicheng district ☎ (010) 6618 4917 ⏱ Lunch, dinner

Lao Hanzi ($$)

Sample the cuisine of China's 'guest people', the Hakkas. Try tasty *meicai kourou* (fatty pork with preserved vegetables) or *zhuyan xia* (shrimp cooked in rock salt).

✉ 12 Shichahai Dong'an, 20m north of Pingan Dadao, Xicheng District ☎ (010) 6404 2259 ⏱ Lunch, dinner

Quan Ju De ($$)

No one does Peking duck better than this famous – if slightly expensive – old restaurant. The bird is wheeled to the table and its crispy skin expertly sliced off in front of you.

✉ 32 Qianmen Dajie, Chongwen district ☎ (010) 6511 2418 ⏱ Lunch and dinner

Red Capital Club ($$$)

Excellent Chinese cuisine served in a restored courtyard house. The dishes are said to be the favourites of China's top leaders. The bar is decorated with Cultural Revolution artefacts.

✉ 66 Dongsi Jiutiao, Dongcheng district ☎ (010) 8401 8886 ⏱ Dinner only

South Silk Road (Chama Gudao) ($$)

Spicy, earthy Yunnan food served in a hip restaurant.

✉ 3rd Floor, Building D, Soho (Xiandaicheng) ☎ (010) 8580 4286

CHENGDE
Imperial City Restaurant ($$$)

Very expensive, with but wild game dishes, including wild deer, rabbit and pheasant, fit for Qing emperors.

✉ 4–5 Imperial City, Shanzhuang Lu, between Lizhengmen and Dehuimen Gate, Imperial Villa ☎ (0314) 203 1919 ⏱ Lunch, dinner

DATONG
Yonghe Meishicheng Restaurant ($$)
This slightly (for Datong) classy restaurant offers a wide variety of Chinese dishes. Picture menu makes ordering easier.
✉ 3 Yingbin Donglu ☎ (0352) 510 3008 🕐 Lunch, dinner

HARBIN
Huamei Xicanting ($)
An 80-year-old restaurant with the finest Russian cuisine in town.
✉ 112 Zhongyang Dajie (opposite the Modern Hotel) ☎ (0415) 8461 9818 🕐 Lunch, dinner

PINGYAO
Yunjingcheng Binguan ($$–$$$)
Sample Shanxi dishes including fried buns stuffed with *jianbao* (meat), or the local noodles in this courtyard restaurant and hotel.
✉ Mingqing Dajie, opposite the Xietongqing Museum ☎ (0354) 568 0944; www.pibc.com 🕐 Lunch, dinner

XI'AN
Laosun Jia Restaurant ($$)
This well-known restaurant specializes in Muslim and Xi'an dishes, including *yangrou paomo* (bread and lamb cooked in broth).
✉ 364 Dongda Jie ☎ (029) 8721 4438 🕐 Lunch, Dinner

SHOPPING

ARTS AND CRAFTS
Beijing Antique City (Beijing Guwan Cheng)
With more than 200 stalls, the choice of antiques is immense. Some are genuinely old, others perhaps just created last week.
✉ 21 Dongsanhuannan Lu, Chaoyang District, Beijing ☎ (010) 5960 9999

Beijing Yihong Carpet Factory
The showrooms here are filled with old carpets and rugs from Mongolia, Tibet and Xinjiang.
✉ 35 Juzhang Hutong, Fahuasi Jie, Chongwen District (near the Hongqiao Market), Beijing ☎ (010) 6712 2195 🕐 Mon–Fri 9–5, Sat–Sun 10–5

Hongqiao Market
Also known as the Pearl Market, in addition to fresh water pearls
and other jewellery, Hongqiao also sells a wide variety of
handicrafts and name brand copies.
✉ 46 Tiantan Donglu (close to the east gate of the Temple of Heaven),
Chongwen District, Beijing ☎ (010) 6713 3354

Liulichang
Curio and book shops in a remodelled Qing Dynasty street.
✉ One block south and east of the Xuanwumen subway station, Beijing

Panjiayuan Folk Culture Market
An amazing collection of items are sold in this indoor market:
everything from genuine antiques to copies: handicrafts, paintings,
porcelain, religious art, minority crafts, etc. Has an outdoor section
on Saturdays and Sundays which opens around sunrise. Go early.
✉ Panjiayuan Lu, just inside the east third ring road, close to the Panjiayuan
Bridge, Beijing ☎ (010) 6775 2405

Ruifuxiang Silk and Fabric Store
Find raw silk in a dazzling array of colours, textures and
patterns.The store has been in business for more than a century
and used to serve Qing royalty.
✉ 5 Dazhanlan Jie, Xuanwu district, Beijing ☎ (010) 6303 5312 ⏰ 9–10

ART GALLERIES
Courtyard Gallery
Paintings and sculptures by well-known contemporary Chinese
artists are displayed in the modern courtyard house which is home
to the gallery.
✉ 319 Caochangdi, Chaoyang District, Beijing ☎ (010) 6526 8882

BOOKS AND MUSIC
Wangfujing Xinhua Bookstore
Here you'll find plenty of English-language books, maps and
postcards to browse through.
✉ 218 Wangfujing Dajie (beside Oriental Plaza), Beijing ☎ (010) 6513 2842

SHOPS, MALLS AND DEPARTMENT STORES
China World Trade Centre
Large, all-purpose shopping complex. It reckons it's 'the number one shopping address in China'. Plenty of beautiful textile shops and a fine selection of antique stores.

✉ 1 Jianguomenwai Dajie, Chaoyang District, Beijing ☎ (010) 6505 2288
🕐 Daily 9:30–9:30 (approx)

Outlets Shopping Centre
Good spot to pick up inexpensive clothes.

✉ 9 Dongsihuan Nanlu, Chaoyang District, Beijing ☎ (010) 6739 5678

Oriental Plaza
Beijing's biggest shopping mall, located on the corner of Wangfujing Dajie and Dong Chang'an Jie.

✉ 1 Dong Chang'an Jie, Beijing ☎ (010) 8518 6363; www.orientalplaza.com
🕐 Daily 9:30am–10pm

Silk Market Plaza
A large collection of name brand copies, factory seconds, silk items and handicrafts. Check your purchase carefully for defects and get set to bargain hard.

✉ Xiushui Dongjie, just east of Yonganli metro station, Chaoyang District, Beijing ☎ (010) 5169 8800

SHOPPING STREETS
Qianmen Dajie and Dazhalan, Beijing
This has long been famous as a shopping mecca. The small streets that cut across this area are crowded with small shops, many selling traditional items, such as silk and cloth.

Wangfujing Dajie, Beijing
Although this old street, once Beijing's premier shopping area, has been renovated, with much of it taken up by new upscale shopping malls, it still has a large selection of interesting small and old shops. The first few blocks have now been closed to most traffic, and so it's a great place for a stroll and window-shopping.

ENTERTAINMENT

ARTS

Laoshe Teahouse

Featuring opera, magic tricks and acrobatics. The opera shows are usually enlivened with comedy routines.

✉ 3 Qianmenxi Dajie, Chongwen District, Beijing ☎ (010) 6303 6830; www.laosheteahouse.com 🕔 Daily 7:40 and 9:20pm

✋ Moderate–Expensive

Liyuan Theatre

This has now become Beijing's leading opera house. Screens alongside the stage show English translations and this certainly helps you appreciate what is going on.

✉ Qianmen Hotel, 175 Yongan Lu, Xuanwu District, Beijing ☎ (010) 6301 6688 ext 8860 🕔 Daily 7:30–8:40pm

Sanwei Bookstore

Traditional Chinese music performed by some of Beijing's best classical musicians in a rustic teashop. Reservations are recommended.

✉ 60 Fuxingmennei Dajie, Xicheng District, Beijing ☎ (010) 6601 3204
🕔 Sat 8:30–10:30pm ✋ Moderate

Zhongguo Mu'ou Juyuan

The ancient art of Chinese shadow and hand puppetry is kept alive here at the China Puppet Art Theatre. Troupes from all over China regularly visit for shows. Performances weeekends only.

✉ 1 Anhuaxili, Chaoyang District, Beijing ☎ (010) 6425 4847; www.puppetchina.com (in Chinese) 🕔 Sat 10:30am and 3pm, Sun 3pm

NIGHTLIFE

CD Café

Live music performed by local and foreign jazz and rock groups. CD Café is widely named as one of Beijing's top venues for enjoying live rock.

✉ Dongsanhuan Beilu, south of the Agricultural Exhibition Centre, Chaoyang District, Beijing ☎ (010) 6506 8288 🕔 Daily 3–late

Banana

A loud and raucous nightclub on the first floor, with a much quieter chill-out area above. Banana regularly attracts a string of international DJs.

✉ Scietch Hotel, 22 Jianguomenwai Dajie, Chaoyang district ☎ (010) 6528 3636 ◷ Daily 8:30pm–4am ✋ Cover charge of between 20–30RMB

Guangfuguan Greenhouse

Maybe the best of the many bars along the bohemian Yandai Xiejie street, this unpretentious venue is housed within a converted Taoist temple and is just a stone's throw from Houhai lake.

✉ 37 Yandai Xiejie, Xicheng District ☎ (010) 6404 2778

SPORT

Beijing International Golf Club (Ming Tombs Golf Course)

About one hour from the centre of Beijing, this is considered to be the capital's best course.

✉ North of Shisanling Reservoir, Changping County ☎ (010) 6076 2288

Capital Gymnasium

A venue that features badminton, table tennis, basketball and a climbing centre.

✉ 54 Zhongguancunnan Dajie, Haidian District, Beijing ☎ (010) 8831 8421 ◷ Daily 8am–10pm

China World Fitness Centre

Pay a visit to enjoy the squash courts, indoor tennis courts and the swimming pool.

✉ China World Trade Centre, 1 Jianguomenwai Dajie, Chaoyang District, Beijing ☎ (010) 6505 2266 ◷ Daily 6am–11pm

Nanshan Ski Resort

The largest ski resort in the Beijing area with some of the most advanced facilities in the country. The 18 runs cater to all abilities, though the snow is man-made.

✉ Shengshuitou Village, Miyun County, Beijing ☎ (010) 8909 1909; www.nanshanski.com

Shanghai and Eastern China

Eastern China is home to some of China's most fascinating cities. Foremost among them is Shanghai, a city swaggering fearlessly into the future and dragging the rest of the country along with it. Then there's the refined beauty and traditional architecture of China's 'southern capital', Nanjing. Nearby Suzhou is known as the 'Venice of the East', famed for its canals and its exquisite gardens. And not to forget Hangzhou, the most beautiful city in the world, according to Marco Polo, and still looking lovely thanks to the eternally idyllic West Lake.

☐ Shanghai

The Grand Canal, segments of which date back 2,500 years, traces a path through the region. It may have decayed over the centuries, but remains the longest man-made waterway in the world, stretching 1,610km (1,000 miles). Eastern China also has two of the country's most scenic mountains – Taishan, in Shandong, and Huangshan, both in Anhui province.

SHANGHAI

Shanghai is a relatively young city in terms of Chinese history. Prior to the Treaty of Nanjing and the opening of the five treaty ports in 1842, Shanghai was a humble fishing village near the mouth of the Yangtze River. This all changed, however, when British, French and American settlers teamed up with enterprising Chinese merchants to turn Shanghai into a cosmopolitan city and centre of commerce. During the city's 1920s and 1930s heyday, successful entrepreneurs and celebrities from around the world – such as the playwright Noel Coward and actor Charlie Chaplin – mixed it up in the local hotels, restaurants and clubs.

Time stood still for three decades following liberation in 1949, as the communist leadership warily viewed the city's decadent past and reputation for freewheeling capitalism. When China opened its doors to the outside world in the late 1970s, Shanghai was a pale

shadow of its past self. The Shanghainese, who pride themselves in being the most savvy and enterprising people in China, lost no time in seeking to revive the city's glory. Shanghai underwent a massive transformation, seemingly building overnight state-of-the-art skyscrapers and modern expressways to speed traffic around the bustling city. China's first stock exchange opened here in 1990, and in Pudong, the land east of the Huangpu River, a modern economic zone and thriving commercial centre has risen from land that was previously used for farming little more than 20 years or so ago.

China's most cosmopolitan and densely populated cities, Shanghai's bustling streets are today packed with life. Crowds rush in all directions, beeping cars vie for space on busy streets, and gleaming new department stores overflow with a variety of consumer goods.

 6G

Faguo Zujie (French Concession)

Following the signing of the Treaty of Nanjing in 1842, areas of Shanghai were turned over to the foreign powers for trading purposes, and came to be known as concessions. The French Concession, in the area around Huaihai Lu and the Jinjiang Hotel, had its own buses and trams, electricity, judicial system and traffic regulations.

The heart of the old concession was Avenue Joffre, now known as Huaihai Lu, still the city's premier mecca for shoppers. The area has reminders of its colourful past. It is the best area to wine, dine and generally have a good time in Shanghai. And Fuxing Park, laid out in a Parisian style with wide paths flanked by trees, remains one of the loveliest parks in the city.

✉ Huaihai Lu Zhonglu 🚇 Several stops, including three along Huaihai Lu 🚌 911, 42

Huangpu Jiang (Huangpu River Tour)

The Huangpu River, just 110km (68 miles) long, runs from Lake Taihu and empties into the Yangtze River some 28km (17 miles) downstream from the centre of Shanghai. In the past, large ships would enter the Yangtze, make the short journey along the deep channel of the Huangpu and unload their cargo at the wharves

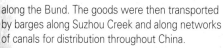

along the Bund. The goods were then transported by barges along Suzhou Creek and along networks of canals for distribution throughout China.

The Huangpu boat tours leave from the southern end of the Bund.

✉ 239 Zhongshan Dong Erlu ☎ (021) 6374 4461; www.pujiangyoulan.com 🕓 Daily 9:30–9:30, sailings every 30 minutes ✋ Moderate 🚇 Nanjing Donglu

Nanjing Lu (Nanjing Road)

Shanghai's most famous street, Nanjing Lu, was once known as the Dama Lu, or 'Great Horse Road'. Although now rivalled by Huaihai Lu as a centre of commerce it is still hugely popular with shoppers.
Nanjing Donglu (Nanjing Road East), the most lively section, begins at People's Square and runs past pre-war shops, department stores, and modern boutiques all the way to the Bund, on the banks of the Huangpu River. Where Nanjing Donglu meets Nanjing Xilu is the old racecourse grandstand and clock, and the Park Hotel, the tallest building outside the Americas at the time of construction in 1934.

🚇 Nanjing Donglu 🚌 11, 14, 26

a walk around the Bund and Nanjing Lu

Start your walk at the Park Hotel, roughly where Nanjing Donglu meets Nanjing Xilu at the north of People's Square. Turn left out of the hotel and stroll past buildings that date from the concession days, including the old Wing On and Sincere department stores. After about half an hour you will pass the imposing, Gothic Peace Hotel on your left before emerging onto the Bund, with the Huangpu River just across the way.

Of the many families of Sephardic Jews that flourished in pre-war Shanghai, the best known is the Sassoon family. The family fled from Baghdad in the 18th century to make a new life in Bombay and then proceeded to buy wharf space in Shanghai. Victor Sassoon built the Peace Hotel, a landmark on Nanjing Lu and many skyscrapers have copied its distinctive pyramidal roof design. Today's Peace Hotel dates from 1930, with the Gothic façade looking like

something out of boom-era Chicago. The furnishings were spectacular and the Horse and Hounds Bar was the most fashionable rendezvous point in the city. The glory faded throughout the rest of the 20th century and the hotel became so worn that, in early 2007, a major renovation was launched.

Continue on to the Bund. Turn left, passing pre-World War II European buildings, including the original headquarters of the former opium traders, Jardine Matheson, and the old

British Consulate. At the Waibaidu Bridge cross to the riverside embankment and return along the Bund. Walk south to the end of the Bund, just opposite the Dong Feng Hotel, the old Shanghai Club, and re-cross the road before walking the short distance to Bund 5 (5 Zhongshan Dongyi Lu), home to the M on the Bund restaurant.

Distance: 4km (2.5 miles) **Time:** 2 hours
Start point: The Park Hotel
End point and lunch: M on the Bund ($$$)
Lunch: Dragon-Phoenix Restaurant, Peace Hotel ($$)
✉ 7th Floor, 5 Zhongshan Dongyi Lu (entrance at 20 Guangdong Lu
☎ (021) 6350 9988; www.m-restaurantgroup.com
🕐 Daily (except Mon lunch)

Nanshi (Shanghai Old Town)

Before 1842, Shanghai was a walled town concentrated in the area sometimes called Nanshi in the Huangpu District. Unfortunately, the walls were pulled down in 1911 but modern day Renmin Lu still reflects the circular shape of the old edifice. The centre of the town was dominated by the Huxinting Teahouse, Yu Garden (► 120–121), and the Temple of the City God. The maze of alleyways within Renmin Lu is an ideal place to experience old Shanghai. Huxingting Tea House, in the centre of the lake, is 18th-century. The teahouse is approached via Nine Zig-Zag Bridge.

🖂 Huangpu District, southwest of the Bund

Pudong

Pudong, literally translated as 'east of the Huangpu River', is Shanghai's impresssive new financial and commercial district. The area is linked to old Shanghai, Puxi, by a series of bridges and tunnels, including the charmingly kitsch Tourist Tunnel. The area is home to the 468m (1,536ft) Oriental Pearl TV Tower, which gives panoramic views of Shanghai. The stunning **Jinmao Tower** houses the Grand Hyatt Hotel, the highest hotel in the world. Meanwhile Shanghai World Financial Centre has gone a few storeys better and now claims to be the tallest building in China.

Jinmao Tower

🖂 2 Shiji Dadao, Pudong 🕿 (021) 5047 0088, ext 5304 🕓 Daily 8:30–9:30 ✋ Moderate 🚇 Lujiazui

Shanghai Bowuguan (Shanghai Museum)

The impressive Shanghai Museum is without a doubt the best-designed and most modern museum in all of China.

Formally opened in 1996 on People's Square, the museum houses some 120,000 cultural relics, displayed to their best advantage by state-of-the-art lighting. The three principal permament galleries to visit are bronzes and stone sculptures, ceramics and paintings.

Other galleries are devoted to jade, Chinese coins, seals, calligraphy, traditional furniture and the art of China's minority peoples. There are also special temporary exhibition halls.

✉ 201 Renmin Dadao, Huangpu District
☎ (021) 6372 3500; www.shanghaimuseum.net
🕙 Daily 9–4 ✋ Inexpensive
🚇 Renmin Square
🚌 23, 49

Soong Qingling Guju (Soong Qingling's Residence)

Soong Qingling was born in Shanghai in 1893, the daughter of Charlie Soong, a publisher of Bibles and a supporter of Sun Yatsen's revolution against the Qing Dynasty. After being educated in the US, Soong worked for Sun as his secretary, later marrying him. After Sun's death, Soong became disillusioned with Chiang Kaishek, the successor to Sun, and threw her support behind the Chinese Communists. After the communist victory, Soong held a number of posts in the government, becoming a symbol for China until her death in 1981.

✉ 1843 Huaihaizhong Lu ☎ (021) 6474 7183 🕔 Daily 9–4:30
💵 Inexpensive 🚇 Hengshan Lu 🚌 911, 42

Sun Zhongshan Guju (Sun Yatsen's Residence)

Sun moved to this small house, located on what was then known as Rue Molière in the French Concession, in 1920 with his young wife Soong Qingling, remaining here until his death in 1925. Considered the Father of the Chinese Republic, Sun Yatsen helped to overthrow the Qing Dynasty in 1911. As the Nationalist Party leader, he struggled against warlord factions to try to unite China, later helped by the Soviet Union and the Chinese Communist Party.

✉ 7 Xiangshan Lu ☎ (021) 6437 2954
🕔 Daily 9–4:30 💵 Inexpensive
🚇 Shanxi Nanlu 🚌 24, 41

Xujiahui Tianzhu Jiaotang (St Ignatius Cathedral)

Xu Guangqi, a native of Xujiahui, or Xu Family Village, and an official of the Imperial Library, was an early convert to Catholicism. Baptised Paul, he later donated family land to Jesuit missionaries from Europe for the construction of an observatory and a cathedral. Following a period of anti-Catholic persecution, the church was turned into a temple dedicated to the God of War. After the Treaty of Nanjing (1842) the land was turned over to the French, and two years later a Jesuit settlement was established here. The present structure, St Ignatius Cathedral, was built in 1906 with two 50m-tall (164ft) spires and a capacity for 2,500. The interior includes traces of Buddhist symbolizm: melons on the nave columns and stylised bats on the windows. Severely damaged during the Cultural Revolution, the cathedral has been restored and is now a functioning church again, with daily Mass.

✉ 158 Puxi Lu ☎ (021) 6253 0959 🕑 Services Mon–Sat 6:15am and 7am, Sun 6am, 7:30am, 10am and 6pm (all services in Chinese) Ⓜ Xujiahui 🚌 42, 50

Yu Yuan (Yu Garden)

Yu Garden was created in the mid-16th century by Pan Yunduan as an act of filial affection for his father. Pan, a Shanghai native who had been in public service in Sichuan Province, must have been a wealthy figure in the city, for the garden takes up almost 5ha (12 acres). Following the death of the elder Pan in 1577, the garden fell into neglect. It was used twice as a military headquarters in the 19th century, first by Lieutenant General Gough of the British Land Force in 1842, and in the 1850s by the Small Sword Society, an offshoot of the secret Heaven and Earth Society.

The garden is a fine example of a classic Ming garden, with rock gardens, bridges and ponds surrounding pavilions and corridors to create an illusion of a natural landscape.

✉ 132 Anren Jie, Huangpu District 🕐 Daily 8:30–4:45 ✋ Moderate
🚌 11, 126

Xiantiandi

Since opening in 2001, Xintiandi has become Shanghai's most fashionable funhouse. Crafted from a 1930s shikumen (stone-gate dwelling) estate, Xiantiandi is festooned with bars, restaurants and nightclubs. The history of the area and significance of the buildings is explained in detail in the Shikumen House Museum (daily 10–10). The other museum is the Site of the 1st National Congress of the Chinese Communist Party (daily 9–4), located in the very house in which the CCP was secretly founded in 1921 and now part of Shanghai's most trendy and fashionable enclave.

✉ Huangpi Nanlu, Luwan District ☎ (021) 6311 2288 🚇 Huangpi Nanlu
ℹ Opposite the Shikumen Museum

Anhui and Henan Provinces

HUANGSHAN (YELLOW MOUNTAIN)

Located in southern Anhui Province, Huangshan is considered one of China's most scenic mountain areas. According to legend, Emperor Minghuang of the Tang Dynasty believed the Yellow Emperor, Qin Shi Huang, made immortality pills on the mountain, then called Yishan. The name was thus changed to its present one. The mountain's rising craggy peaks inspired a genre of landscape painting.

🕂 5H ✉ 70km (43 miles) north of Huangshan City
🖐 Expensive 🚆 Daily overnight train (N418) from Shanghai to Huangshan City ✈ Huangshan Airport (5km/3 miles west of Huangshan City)

LUOYANG

Luoyang served as the capital and cultural centre for 10 Dynasties, covering a period of more than 1,000 years. The city was destroyed by wars, but was rebuilt many times. Luoyang expanded rapidly during the Han Dynasty, propelled by the invention of paper and the introduction of Buddhism from India, which led to some 1,300 temples being built in the city. Luoyang also boasted an impressive imperial university and library, which

attracted tens of thousands of scholars. These days the city is largely industrial however, tourists still flock here for the Longmen Caves, one of China's most important and spectacular Buddhist grottoes.

🕂 3F ✉ 90km (56 miles) west of Zhengzhou, Henan Province 🚌 Buses to Beijing, Kaifeng, Zhengzhou 🚆 Daily from Beijing, Shanghai, Xi'an, Zhengzhou ✈ Luoyang Airport (12km/7.5 miles north of the city)

SHAOLIN TEMPLE

Fêted as the birthplace of China's fighting arts, Shaolin Temple dates back to AD497 and occupies a scenic spot on the western edge of Songshan, one of Taoism's five sacred mountains. Legend has it that Shaolin Boxing was developed here by Bodhidharma, a south Asian ascetic and the founder of Zen Buddhism, who began to imitate animals as a means of relaxation between meditation sessions. These exercises evolved into the 'kungfu' we know today. Visit the Qianfo (Thousand Buddha) hall to see where resident monks have practised their moves for centuries and walk among the delightful Stupa Forest where hundreds of pagodas commemorate eminent monks.

 3F ✉ 80km (50 miles) southwest of Zhengzhou, Henan Province
☎ (0371) 6274 8971 ⏲ Daily 7–6:30 ✋ Expensive
🚌 Buses to Luoyang and Zhengzhou

Jiangsu Province

NANJING

One of China's four ancient capital cities, Nanjing was once known as 'a home of emperors and kings'. Strategically located on the southern bank of the Yangze River, it served as capital during the Three Kingdoms period, the Song, Liang and Tang Dynasties. It became China's capital again for a brief period in the Ming Dynasty, and again after 1928 when Chiang Kaishek moved his struggling Nationalist government here. Japanese troops invaded the city in 1937, committing one of the 20th century's worst atrocities.The so-called Rape of Nanjing left an estimated 300,000 Chinese dead. When the Communists came to power in 1949, the capital was once again moved back to Beijing.

Much of the Ming City Wall (at 42km/26 miles in length, the longest in China) still stands, including the impressive Heping and Zhonghua gates. The double-decker Nanjing River Bridge, which

crosses the Yangze River, is also worthy of a look. In the centre of the city is the Drum Tower, built in 1382, and the Bell Tower, which houses a huge bronze bell, cast in 1388. Nearby Zijinshan (Purple and Gold Mountain) is home to many tourist sights, including Sun Yatsen's huge mausoleum, the tomb of Huangwu, first emporer of the Ming dynasty, and a working astronomical observatory.

✚ 5G ✉ Capital of Jiangsu Province, 300km (186 miles) northwest of Shanghai 🚌 Express buses to Hangzhou, Shanghai, Suzhou 🚆 Daily from Beijing, Hangzhou, Shanghai, Wuxi

SUZHOU

Called the Venice of the East, Suzhou is a city of canals, arched bridges, whitewashed houses and ornamental gardens. It has a history of 2,500 years, but did not prosper until the construction of the Grand Canal during the Sui Dynasty (AD581–618). By the 12th century, Suzhou had become a noted producer of silk. It has long been known as a centre for artists, scholars, merchants, financiers and high-ranking government officials who built fine gardens around their villas where they could enjoy a peaceful retirement. The city was damaged when Taiping soldiers occupied it from 1860 to 1863, but it was rebuilt.

The gardens were designed as small replicas of the natural world, with ponds and hills representing famous lakes and mountains. They also included villas, courtyards, covered walkways, pavilions and towers, surrounded by secluding walls.

✚ 5G ✉ 80km (50 miles) west of Shanghai, Jiangsu Province
🚌 Express buses to Hangzhou, Nanjing, Shanghai, Wuxi, Zhouzhuang
🚆 Regular trains throughout the day from Shanghai, also Beijing daily
ℹ North Bus Station, 29 Xihui Beilu ☎ (0512) 6751 6376

ZHOUZHUANG

The old town of Zhouzhuang, with quaint traditional houses standing over arched bridges and canals, lies 35km (22 miles) southwest of Suzhou. The town dates back to 1086 when a noted Buddhist, Zhou Digong, donated 13ha (32 acres) of land to the Full Fortune Temple, which later took the name of Zhouzhuang. Around 60 per cent of the houses are said to date back to the Ming and Qing dynasties. For a tour of the picturesque city, explore the small alleyways or take a ride in one of the boats that follow the canals.

➕ 5G ✉ 35km southwest of Suzhou, Jiangsu Province
☎ (0512) 5721 1654; www.zhouzhuang.net ✋ Expensive
🚌 Regular buses from Suzhou and Shanghai Sightseeing Bus Centre (inside Shanghai Stadium)

Shandong Province

QINGDAO

Best places to see, ➤ 52–53.

TAISHAN

Taishan is one of the five sacred Taoist mountains in China. Revered for more than 2,500 years, 72 emperors performed rituals here. Since Taishan is the farthest east of the sacred mountains, the Chinese believed that the sun began its daily trip westward from here. The climb to the top includes 7,000 stone steps leading to the 1,560m (5,118ft) summit, or there is a cable car. Over the centuries, more than 250 Taoist and Buddhist temples and monuments were built here.

➕ 4E ✉ Tai'an City, 64km (40 miles) north of Qufu, Shandong Province ✋ Expensive 🚌 Regular services from Jinan and Qufu
🚉 Tai'an Railway Station 🚌 Minibuses from Qufu

QUFU

The birthplace of Confucius (551–479BC), Qufu was the capital of the state of Lu at the time of the Master's birth. After the death of Confucius, Emperor Han Wudi built a temple to honour the great Master. Today, about 100,000 of the city's more than 500,000 residents claim the Kong family name (Confucius' surname was Kong). Imperial allowances stopped in 1911 when the Qing Dynasty was overthrown, and most of the Kong family were forced to flee the city when the Communists came to power in 1949. The adjacent Kong Family Mansion is where family members lived until 1937. The mansion was first built in 1068, but the present structures were built in the Ming and Qing dynasties. The Apricot Altar is the site where Confucius taught his students.

The Confucius Cemetery, north of Qufu, is the site of some 100,000 Kong tombs, with Confucius buried in the centre of the cemetery. His son,

Kong Li, is buried to the east, and his grandson to the south.

🚻 4F ✉ Shandong Province 🚌 Buses to Yanzhou 16km (10 miles) to the west, Tai'an, Jinan and Qingdao
🚉 Yanzhou
❓ The Confucius Cultural Festival, 26 Sep–10 Oct

Zhejiang Province

HANGZHOU

Hangzhou, an old imperial capital, is renowned for its serene beauty. Marco Polo, who visited here in the 13th century, called it the most beautiful and prosperous city in the world. Many artists flocked here, transforming it into a cultural centre. Two of China's most famous poets, Tang poet Bai Juyi and Song poet Su Dongpo, served as mayors. Hangzhou continued to prosper during the Ming and Qing eras due to the thriving silk industry and its location in a fertile rice-growing region. The city was attacked by pirates in the 16th century, and was damaged during the Taiping Rebellion in the 19th century.

The main tourist attraction is West Lake, which is encircled by misty green hills where Longjing tea and mulberry trees are cultivated. Originally a humble lagoon, West Lake was dredged in the 8th century and later diked. It is one of the few attractions in China that you won't need to pay for the pleasure of viewing. The Su Causeway, named after Su Dongpo, is a good place to enjoy the lake's scenery.

The Tomb and Temple of Yue Fei, a Song Dynasty general and patriot who was unjustly executed, lies on the northern shore of lake. To the west of the lake is Lingyin Temple whose origins date back to AD326. Just behind is Bei Gaofeng (Northern Peak) which affords a sweeping view of lake and city.

✚ 5H ✉ Capital of Zhejiang Province, 175km (109 miles) southwest of Shanghai 🍴 Louwailou ($$) 🚌 Express buses to Nanjing, Shanghai
🚆 Daily from Shanghai (throughout the day), Beijing, Guangzhou
✈ Hangzhou Airport (15km/9 miles) from city centre
ℹ Hangzhou Railway Station ☎ (0571) 8782 5755

PUTUOSHAN

Putuoshan, one of the four sacred Buddhist mountains, is a hilly island about 6km (4 miles) long and 5km (3 miles) wide, with its highest point the 286m-tall (938ft) Buddha's Peak. The island is known for its views and temples, immortalized by Chinese artists. There are two main temples here. The Puji Temple in the south was built in the 16th century, and was later enlarged in the 17th century. The Huiji Temple in the north is smaller, but more interesting as it is built on a series of terraces on the slope of Buddha's Peak. A large lacquered wood, gold covered sculpture of Guanyin, the Goddess of Mercy, is in the Ninth Dragon Hall.

✚ 6H ✉ Zhejiang Province, East China Sea 💧 Expensive 🚢 Regular boats from Ningbo, daily overnight boat from Shanghai

HOTELS

HANGZHOU
Shangri-La Hotel ($$$)
Beautifully located amid lush gardens and overlooking Hangzhou's
famed West Lake. With a fitness centre, snooker and billiards hall,
swimming pool and sauna this is the best-equipped hotel in town.
✉ 78 Beishan Lu ☎ (0571) 8797 7951; www.shangri-la.com

HUANGSHAN
Beihai Binguan ($$)
The best hotel for those wanting to catch the sunrise or sunset
from the top of the mountain. It's a 20-minute walk away from the
White Goose Peak cable car. Facilities are adequate.
✉ Beihai Scenic Area, eastern steps of the mountain ☎ (0559) 558 2555;
www.beihaihotel.com

LUOYANG
Peony Hotel ($$)
Located at the heart of Luoyang this hotel has attractive, spacious
rooms with satellite television and air-conditioning. Other facilities
include a sauna and an excellent restaurant, the Mudan Ting.
✉ 15 Zhongzhou Xilu ☎ (0379) 6468 0000

NANJING
Jinling Fandian ($$–$$$)
Probably the best local hotel in town, located in the very heart of
bustling Nanjing. Swimming pool, sauna and steam room,
shopping arcade and a number of excellent restaurants.
✉ 2 Hanzhong Lu, Xinjiekou Square ☎ (025) 8471 1888;
www.jinlinghotel.com

QINGDAO
Shangri-La Hotel ($$$)
In the east of the town, this typically plush and elegant member of
the elite Shangri-La chain has an indoor pool, fitness centre, tennis
courts and the famed Shang Palace Cantonese restaurant.
✉ 9 Xianggang Zhonglu ☎ (0532) 8388 3838; www.shangri-la.com

QUFU
Queli Hotel ($–$$)
Located just a stone's throw from the famous Confucian Temple. The staff greet visitors with one of Confucius' famous quotes, 'It is wonderful to have friends from afar!' All rooms have satellite television and minibar.

✉ 1 Queli Jie ☎ (0537) 486 6818; www.quelihotel.com

PUTUOSHAN
Sanshengtang Fandian ($)
This used to be a huge monastery. Facilities are limited, but it's a good starting point for walks around the island.

✉ 121 Miaozhuangyan Lu ☎ (0580) 609 1277

SHANGHAI
Grand Hyatt ($$$)
The Jinmao Tower is the third tallest building in the world and the Hyatt starts on the 53rd floor. The inner atrium stretches up to the tower's viewing level. The hotel boasts extensive spa facilities, indoor swimming pool, sauna and a weight room.

✉ Jinmao Tower, 88 Shiji Dadao, Pudong ☎ (021) 5049 1234; www.shanghai.hyatt.com

Peace Hotel ($$$)
Shanghai's classic old hotel situated right on the Bund. You get a real sense of history walking its corridors. Facilities are not as extensive as they should be for a hotel of this standing, but easy access to Nanjing Lu and the Bund make up for this.

✉ 20 Nanjingdong Lu ☎ (021) 6321 6888; www.shanghaipeacehotel.com

The Portman Ritz-Carlton ($$$)
Winner of numerous 'Best Hotel' awards this giant, 564-room hotel caters to all tastes. Health club, large shopping mall and 24-hour business centre. Also houses the renowned Summer Pavilion Chinese Restaurant.

✉ Shanghai Centre, 1376 Nanjingxi Lu ☎ (021) 6279 8888; www.ritzcarlton.com

Ruijin Guesthouse ($$)

Located within the former walled estate of colonial newspaper magnate, H E Morris, the Ruijin Guesthouse consists of a series of converted 1920s villas surrounding a garden. Also on the estate is Face bar and the celebrated Xiao Nan Guo restaurant.

✉ 118 Ruijin Erlu, Luwan District ☎ (021) 6472 5222;
www.shedi.net.cn/outedi/ruijin

SUZHOU
Bamboo Grove Hotel ($–$$)

Despite boasting its own garden, the Bamboo Grove Hotel is well located for many of Suzhou's more famous gardens. Comfortable and friendly hotel with gym, tennis courts, sauna and swimming pool. Also has non-smoking rooms.

✉ 168 Zuhui Lu ☎ (0512) 6520 5601; www.bg-hotel.com

RESTAURANTS

HANGZHOU
Louwailou ($$)

Located with excellent views of West Lake. Specialties include West Lake *xihu cuyu* (vinegar fish), *dongpo rou* (pork slices cooked with Shaoxing wine), longjing shrimp and beggar's chicken.

✉ 30 Gushan Lu ☎ (0571) 8796 9023; www.louwailou.com.cn
🕐 Lunch, dinner

Zhiweiguan Restaurant ($)

This simple restaurant offers popular local snacks from noodles to boiled and steamed dumplings. Try cat's ears (not what you think) – small triangles of dough snipped off into a boiling pot, and served in a broth.

✉ 83 Renhe Lu ☎ (0571) 870 8638 🕐 Breakfast, lunch and dinner

NANJING
Qinhuai Renjia ($)

Plain cafeteria style eatery on Dashiba Jie, one of the atmospheric 'old streets' close to the Confucius Temple (Fuzi Miao) area.

✉ 128 Dashiba Jie, Fuzi Miao ☎ (025) 5221 1888 🕐 Lunch, dinner

PUTUOSHAN
Zhongshan Fandian ($)
In keeping with the Buddhist spirit of Putuoshan, this restaurant serves up excellent vegetarian food, as well as seafood dishes.
✉ 19 Xiangyun Lu, beside the Fayu Temple, Putuoshan ☎ (0580) 669 0899
🕐 Lunch, dinner

QINGDAO
Tianfu Laoma ($$)
Decorated in a traditional style, this restaurant is a favourite with locals and serves dishes from several of the Chinese schools of cooking, from Sichuan-style hot pot to eastern seafood favourites.
✉ 54 Yunxiao Lu, Shinan District ☎ (0532 8576 4906) 🕐 Lunch, dinner

SHANGHAI
Bi Feng Tang ($)
With branches in various prize locations around Shanghai, this restaurant serves up great value Cantonese Dim Sum dishes in a bright, festive environment. Menus are in English.
✉ 1333 Nanjing Xilu, close to Tongren Lu ☎ (021) 6279 0738
🕐 Breakfast, lunch, dinner

Dongbei Ren ($)
Donbei Ren serves up fun peasant-style food over two crowded storeys. Order the Squirrel Fish and the smart waiting staff will sing and clap as food is bought to your table.
✉ 46 Panyu Lu [by Yanan Xilu] ☎ (021) 5230 2230; www.dongbeiren.com
🕐 Lunch, dinner

Huxingting Tea House ($$)
Serves Shanghai snacks and tea in one of the most attractive classical buildings in the city.
✉ 257 Yuyuan Lu ☎ (021) 6373 6950 🕐 Lunch, dinner

Kathleen's 5 ($$$)
Located on the rooftop of the Shanghai Art Museum, Kathleen's 5 is an elegant restaurant with a casual glassed-in terrace beneath

the clock tower. Superb views over People's Park.

✉ 5th Floor, Shanghai Art Museum, 325 Nanjing Xilu ☎ (021) 6327 2221; www.kathleens5.com.cn 🕓 Lunch, dinner

M on the Bund ($$$)

Haute cuisine served with one of the best views of the waterfront and the Pudong skyline. M on the Bund serves good Mediterranean cuisine. Smart attire a must.

✉ 7th Floor, 5 Zhongshan Dongyi Lu (entrance at 20 Guangdong Lu), Huangpu District ☎ (021) 6350 9988; www.m-restaurantgroup.com 🕓 Lunch, dinner (except Mon lunch)

Sasha's ($$)

Ensconced within a beautiful 1920s French Concession villa, Sasha's offers European food and wine in an elegant setting.

✉ 11 Dongping Lu (near Hengshan Lu) ☎ (021) 6474 6628; www.sashas-shanghai.com 🕓 Lunch, dinner

Yang's Kitchen ($$)

Shanghai home-style cooking in a refined setting.

✉ No 3, Alley 9, Hengshan Lu (near the intersection of Dongping Lu) ☎ (021) 6445 8418 🕓 Lunch, dinner

SUZHOU
Songhelou ($)

The long-established Songhelou is known for its eastern Chinese seafood cooking. Other branches around the city.

✉ 72 Taijian Lu, off Guanqian Jie ☎ (0512) 6727 7006 🕓 Lunch, dinner

SHOPPING

Arts and Crafts Institute

Home to a number of workshops where craftsmen turn out everything from bamboo carvings to inlaid lacquer ware.

✉ 79 Fenyang Lu, Shanghai ☎ (021) 6437 2509 🕓 9–5

Friendship Store

A large selection of interesting, although expensive, antiques,,

porcelain and cloisonné are available at this state-run shop.
✉ 1188 Changshou Lu, Shanghai ☎ (021) 6252 5252

Fuyou Market

Shanghai's most famous antiques market. The best bargains can
be had early mornings at weekends. Bargaining is a must.
✉ Fangbang Zhonglu (near Henan Nanlu), Huangpu District ⏰ Daily 9–5
approx. Open from 5am Sat–Sun

Gu Yue Xuan

An interesting assortment of old clocks and watches at negotiable
prices. Other oddities include beautiful old painted snuff bottles.
✉ 378 Changle Lu, Shanghai ☎ (021) 6218 3316 ⏰ 12:30–10

Hongqiao International Pearl City

Large shopping centre stuffed with smaller vendors who allow you
to commission your own jewellery or buy ready-made items.
✉ 3721 Hongmei Lu (by Yan'an Xilu), Minhang District ☎ (021) 6465 0000;
www.hqpearl.com

Shanghai South Bund Fabric Market

Bespoke clothing can be stitched together amazingly quickly here.
✉ 399 Lujiabang Lu, Huangpu district ☎ (021) 6377 2236 ⏰ Daily 8:30–6

Torana House

This indie shop specializes in handmade wool rugs from Tibet and
parts of the former Silk Road.
✉ No 1, Lane 180 Shanxi Nanlu ☎ (021) 5404 4886; www.toranahouse.com
⏰ Daily 10–9

ART GALLERIES
Shanghai Museum Shop

A large collection of tasteful art reproductions, paintings,
stationary, books and more. Well worth visiting if you're in the
museum.
✉ Shanghai Museum, 201 Renmin Lu, Shanghai ☎ (021) 6372 3500;
www.shanghaimuseum.net

BOOKS
Shanghai Foreign Languages Bookstore
All kinds of foreign language books, primarily English, but some in Spanish, French and other languages, as well as CDs and videos.
✉ 390 Fuzhou Lu, Shanghai ☎ (021) 6322 3200

Garden Books
Sells a wide range of imported titles, as well as international ones. Also has an ice-parlour on the ground floor.
✉ 325 Changle Lu, Shanghai ☎ (021) 5404 8728

DEPARTMENT STORES
Plaza 66
More than 100 designer brands have a home in this trendy mall, close to the Shanghai Centre. Good for an entire day's shopping.
✉ 1266 Nanjing Xilu (near Jiangning Lu) ☎ (021) 6279 0910 🕐 10–10

Isetan
Japanese-run department store on one of Shanghai's main shopping drags. Sells international, Japanese and local products.
✉ 537 Huaihai Zhonglu, Shanghai ☎ (021) 5306 1111 🕐 Mon–Fri 10–9, Sat–Sun 10–9:30

Shanghai No 1 Department Store
This old pre-liberation stalwart has an enormous range of products.
✉ 830 Nanjing Donglu, Shanghai ☎ (021) 6322 3344 🕐 9:30–10

SHOPPING STREETS
Nanjing Donglu, Shanghai
Packed with small shops, boutiques and department stores, this commercial centre is at the heart of modern Shanghai.

ENTERTAINMENT

ARTS
Garden of the Master of the Nets
Nightly performances including traditional local opera, dance and theatre. The audience moves around the gardens.

✉ 11 Kuojiatou Xiang (front gate) or Shiquan Jie (back gate), Suzhou
☎ (0512) 6520 3514 🕐 Daily 7:30–9:30pm

Shanghai Concert Hall

This is the home of the Shanghai Symphony Orchestra. Check local listings magazines for performances.

✉ 523 Yan'an Donglu, Shanghai ☎ (021) 5386 6666; www.culture.sh.cn

Shanghai Dramatic Arts Centre

A small theatre with consistently good productions, and some performances in English. Check the website for current events.

✉ 288 Anfu Lu, Shanghai ☎ (021) 6473 4567; www.china-drama.com

Shanghai Grand Theatre

A huge, superbly designed modern opera house with a spectacular curved roof. The building contains three separate theatres, each welcoming artists from all over the world.

✉ 300 Renmin Dadao, Shanghai ☎ (021) 6386 8686; www.culture.sh.cn

Shanghai Centre Theatre

Home to the Shanghai Acrobatics Troupe who put on a daily hour-and-a-half show. Occasionally the venue for music concerts.

✉ 1376 Nanjing Xilu ☎ (021) 6279 8948 🕐 Shows begin at 7:30pm

Studio City

Large, modern movie hall with six screens showing all the latest blockbusters. Soundtracks in Chinese and English.

✉ 10th Floor Westgate Mall, 1038 Nanjingxi Lu, Shanghai
☎ (021) 6218 2173

Yifu Theatre

A famous old Beijing Opera theatre. Many of the greatest stars of this traditional art have performed here. There are evening performances on Friday and Saturdays with a Sunday matinee.

✉ 701 Fuzhou Lu, Shanghai ☎ (021) 6351 4668; www.tianchan.com

NIGHTLIFE

Old China Hand Reading Room

Bar, café and library all rolled into one. An excellent selection of books on old Shanghai and other subjects. The Old China Hand is decorated with interesting art and antiques, making it a great place to relax with a drink.

✉ 27 Shaoxing Lu, Shanghai ☎ (021) 6473 2526

O'Malley's Irish Pub

This intimate bar, located in an old Shanghai mansion, has an elegant hardwood interior and authentic Irish antiques. An ideal place for enjoying a drink outdoors in the warm weather.

✉ 42 Taojiang Lu, Shanghai ☎ (021) 6474 4533; www.omalleys-shanghai.com

Bar Rouge

Shanghai's classiest cocktail lounge features 33 hand-blown Venetian chandeliers, velvet couches and a fabulous outdoor roof terrace. The trendiest place in town.

✉ 7th Floor, 18 Zhongshan Dongyi Lu ☎ (021) 6339 1199; www.resto18.com
🕓 6:30pm–2am (later on weekends)

SPORT

Disc Kart Indoor Karting

An indoor go-kart racing track covering 4,500sq m (5,382sq yds).

✉ 809 Zaoyang Lu, near Jinshajing Lu line 3 metro station, Shanghai
☎ (021) 6222 2880; www.kartingchina.com 🕓 Daily 2pm–2am

IB Racing Kart Club

Outdoor leisure and racing go-karts.

✉ 880 Zhongshan Beiyilu, inside Quyang Park, Hongkou District, Shanghai
☎ (021) 6531 6800; www.quyangkart.com 🕓 Daily 10–10

Masterhand Rock Climbing Club

Indoor and outdoor rock climbing, mountaineering and camping.

✉ No 21, Upper Stand, Hongkou Football Stadium, 444 Dongjiangwan Lu, Shanghai ☎ (021) 5696 6657 🕓 Daily 10–10

Hong Kong and Southern China

Hong Kong serves up an exotic entrée to the China experience, blending Western comforts with Chinese verve. But there is much more to the southern part of China than this waterfront metropolis.

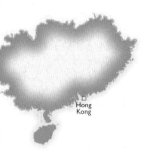

Hong Kong

Known primarily as a city destination, Hong Kong's landscapes are often overlooked. The spectacular skyline of Hong Kong Island contrasts sharply with the rugged wilderness of Lantau Island.

The province that wraps around Hong Kong is Guangdong – crucible of Cantonese culture and home to famously fine food.

Nearby Hainan Island is a tropical treat, blessed with blue skies, great sand beaches and a bevy of beautiful hotels.

Moving deeper into the south, the landscape and inhabitants become more diverse. The provinces of Guangxi and Guizhou boast soaring rice terraces, sugarloaf karst mountains and diverse minority communities, each with their own traditions, costumes, language and culture. Fujian Province has a large Hakka population, distinguished for its unusual architecture. Hunan, meanwhile, sets itself apart with food. Mao Zedong's home province is known for its affection for chilli peppers.

HONG KONG
Best places to see, ➤ 44–45.

Hong Kong Island
What Queen Victoria once assumed to be a useless lump of rock is now the high rise-studded symbol of Asian affluence. The island represents only a fraction of Hong Kong's overall bulk but a lot of money, power and people are packed into its limited confines. The district of Central is where most deals are done. The 88-storey Two IFC office tower dominates the skyline but there are smaller gems worth seeking out, like the Legislative Council Building. Lang Kwai Fong and surrounding streets have the best bars in town, while catching the **Peak Tram** up to Victoria Peak is an essential experience. Also find time to ride the Mid-Levels Escalator up to the trendy Soho district. Sheung Wan is a

more traditionally Chinese district, with musty old shops selling herbal remedies. The southern half of the island is green and hilly with a few quaint seaside towns. Stanley has a great outdoor market, while Aberdeen is home to the Ocean Park centre (➤ 66).

✚ 4L

Peak Tram

✉ 33 Garden Road, Central (behind St John's Building) ☎ (852) 2849 0818
🕐 Daily 7–midnight ✋ Inexpensive 🚌 15, 15B, 15C, 515

Kowloon

Kowloon is the chunk of land to the north of Victoria Harbour. The district at the southern tip is known as Tsim Sha Tsiu, or TST for short, and is home to a cluster of cultural buildings (➤ 143). A little further in land is the excellent **Hong Kong Museum of History.** The maze of streets farther north is a different proposition. The slick sophistication of Hong Kong Island is replaced by a riot of commercialism set against a backdrop of crumbling tenement blocks and crackling neon signs. Nathan Road is the main vein that runs from the waterfront all the way to Boundary Road. Temple Street Market (4pm–midnight), is Hong Kong's most famous night market. Farther north is the **Chi Lin Nunnery,** probably the best free temple in China.

✚ 4L

Chi Lin Nunnery

✉ 5 Chi Lin Drive, Diamond Hill ☎ (852) 2354 1789 🕐 Convent: Daily 9–4,
Lotus Pond Garden: Daily 7–9 ✋ Free 🚇 Diamond Hill

Hong Kong Museum of History

✉ 100 Chatham Road South ☎ (852) 2724 9042 🕐 Mon, Wed–Sat 10–6,
Sun 10–7. Closed Tue ✋ Inexpensive 🚇 Tsim Sha Tsui East KCR

Lantau Island

With its mountainous interior and rocky coastline, Lantau has long been a favourite for outdoor types. It now has mass appeal thanks to a series of tourist developments. First came the **Tian Tan Buddha.** Constructed near Lantau Peak in 1993, the so-called 'Big Buddha' commands great views. The next major development was Hong Kong Disneyland, built on reclaimed land towards Lantau's eastern tip. Most recently, the **Ngong Ping Skyrail** – the world's longest cable car ride – began operations. The 5.7km ride (3.5 miles) ferries visitors up from Tung Chung to the Ngong Ping Village at thrillingly steep angles.

Ngong Ping Village is billed as a 'traditional Chinese village' but features a host of Western chain stores. Elsewhere on Lantau, Mui Wo and Tai O are pleasant fishing villages that offer a different take on Hong Kong life.

➕ 3L

Tian Tan Buddha ✉ Ngong Ping Village ☎ (852) 2985 5248 🕐 10–6 ✋ Free 🚌 2 from Mui Wo, 21 from Tai O, 23 from Tung Chung

Ngong Ping Skyrail
✉ Tung Chung ☎ (852) 2109 9898; www.np360.com.hk 🕐 Mon–Fri 10–6, Sat–Sun 10–6:30 ✋ Moderate 🚇 Tung Chung

Victoria Harbour

This famous passage between Hong Kong Island and Kowloon is now only around half of its original 2km (1.25 miles) width due to extensive land reclamation. Nevertheless, the Star

Ferry ride across the harbour remains one of the world's great boat trips. It may be only nine minutes in duration but the views are breathtaking. Below Central Plaza is the Hong Kong Arts Centre, poking out into the harbour and shaped in a similar bubble fashion to the Sydney Opera House. The Kowloon side of the harbour, meanwhile, is home to another world-class performance venue, the Hong Kong Cultural Centre. The two adjacent buildings, the **Hong Kong Museum of Art** and the **Hong Kong Space Museum** (complete with planetarium) combine to make this Hong Kong's most cultured locale.

✚ 4L

Hong Kong Museum of Art, Hong Kong Space Museum

✉ 10 Salisbury Road, TST ☎ (852) 2721 0116 🕐 Daily 10–6, except Sat 10–8. Closed Thu ✋ Inexpensive (free on Wednesdays) 🚇 Tsim Sha Tsui

Guangdong Province

GUANGZHOU (CANTON)

With its long coastline, Guangdong Province has served as the door for foreigners seeking to penetrate China for more than 1,000 years. Guangzhou, the sprawling provincial capital, today retains traces of its multicultural past in its mix of colonial and traditional Chinese architecture.

Indian and Roman traders sailed up the Pearl River to buy silk, porcelain, tea and spices in the 2nd century. They were followed during the Tang Dynasty by Arab, Jewish, Christian and Zoroastrian merchants and, in the 15th century, by European traders and missionaries. Canton was also the jumping off point for the Chinese who sailed from Southeast Asia and other points in the 19th century. The Qing court attempted to put an end to Britain's lucrative opium trade in 1839, when Commissioner Lin Zexu destroyed opium captured from Western traders. The British quickly routed China in the Opium War, which resulted in the signing of the Treaty of Nanjing, and the opening of Canton and four other cities as treaty ports for foreign trade.

The city of Caton played a key role in the modern revolutionary history of China. The Christian-influenced Taiping Rebellion, which almost succeeded in overthrowing the Qing, was launched here in 1850 by a man claiming to be God's Chinese son. Nationalist hero Sun Yatsen, who was born in nearby Zhongshan, used Canton as a base for a number of uprisings. It also has an important place in modern China. Since Deng Xiaoping's economic reforms were launched in 1979, Guangzhou has been pivotal in driving China's economy upwards.

✚ 3L

Guangxiao Si
(Bright Filial Piety Temple)

This Zen (Chan) Buddhist temple is the oldest in Guangzhou. It was originally the home of a high-ranking official during the Three Kingdoms period, but was turned into a temple following his death. The temple is of special interest because Hui Neng, the Sixth Patriarch of Zen Buddhism, served as a novice monk here in the 600s. The temple has undergone numerous renovations, and most of the present structures date back to 1832 when the most recent renovation was carried out. The Great Hall, with its impressive pillars, is still architecturally interesting. There are two pagodas behind the hall: the stone Jingfa Pagoda built in 676 on top of a hair of Huineng, and the Song Dynasty Eastern Iron Pagoda, made of gilt iron.

✉ Guangxiao Lu

🕐 Daily 6:30–5:30 🚌 56

👆 Inexpensive

Liurongsi Huata
(Six Banyan Trees Temple)

The name of this temple comes from a poem written by Song poet Su Dongpo, who visited the temple in 1100, and was moved by the beauty of the trees in the courtyard, long since disappeared. Su wrote a two-character inscription – six banyans – which is now engraved on a tablet at the entrance. The nine-storey octagonal Flower Pagoda was built in the 11th century.

✉ Liurong Lu 🕑 Daily 9–5:30
🖐 Inexpensive

Shamian Dao (Shamian Island)

This tiny plot of land in the southwest of the city is cleaved from the mainland by little more than a moat. However, cross the footbridge and everything changes: traffic disappears, birdsong strikes up and Guangzhou's hectic mood evaporates. The central boulevard, Shamain Dajie,

runs nearly the width of the island and makes for a pleasant stroll among the examples of French and British architecture. Great views across the Pearl River lure tai chi practitioners at dawn.

✉ South of Liu'ersan Lu

MACAU

The Portuguese leased Macau from China in 1557, and administered it until 1999, when it was returned to China. Composed of a tiny sliver of mainland peninsula and two small islands, Macau was once a booming trade port, but was later eclipsed by nearby Hong Kong. Macau today is a mixture of quaint Portuguese architecture, with interesting old forts, churches and colonial

mansions. It's also become something of an Eastern Las Vagas, thanks to the recent liberalization of the casino industry.

Macau is famous for excellent Portuguese cuisine and laid-back ambience. The stunning façade of St Paul's Cathedral is regarded as the symbol of Macau. Nearby Monte Fort is home to the excellent **Museum of Macau.** The Macanese can now boast their own theme park in the form of **Fisherman's Wharf.** This waterside project features rollercoasters and a flame-erupting volcano 40m (131ft) tall. For those who need their sensory kicks stronger, visit the nearby Macau Tower which has a variety of heart-stopping sky walks and bungee-assisted rides.

✚ 3L ✉ 60km (37 miles) west of Hong Kong 🚢 Regular ferries and hydrofoils from Hong Kong ❓ Macau Arts Festival, Mar

Museum of Macau

✉ Inside Monte Fort ☎ (0853) 2835 7911; www.macau museum.gov.mo
🕐 Tue–Sun 10–6 💰 Inexpensive

Fisherman's Wharf

✉ Avenida Doutor Sun Yat Sen ☎ (853) 299 3300 🕐 Open access

Fujian Province

GULANGYU ISLAND, XIAMEN

Gulangyu served as the headquarters for Zheng Chenggong, the pirate-cum-Ming Dynasty loyalist who drove the Dutch from Taiwan in the 1600s. Foreigners keen to get a foothold in China settled on the island following the First Opium War (1839–1842). The elaborate mansions built by the Europeans remain the big attraction in the area.

Sunlight Rock offers terrific views of the island and its colonial architecture. The Zheng Chenggong Museum houses a collection of historical relics and weapons from the days of Zheng's rule. The Piano Museum has a collection of old pianos from around the world. Take a walk through the bustling main streets and winding alleys, packed with seafood restaurants, old architecture and shops selling local products.

✚ 5K ✉ 5-min ferry ride from Xiamen City 🚌 Electric buses on island
🚃 Xiamen Station ⛴ Ferry from the pier opposite Xiamen's Lujiang Hotel.
Ferry tours along the coast ✈ Xiamen Airport

WUYI SHAN (WUYI MOUNTAIN)

A two-hour trip on a bamboo raft floating downstream from Star Village is the best way to tour picturesque Wuyi Mountain, one of China's 33 UNESCO World Heritage Sites. The journey takes you along the Nine Bends River past soaring peaks, unique rock formations, lush bamboo groves and stunning waterfalls.

The river is also known for the boat-shaped coffins sitting in depressions on the cliffs, said to belong to the Yue, a tribe of people who lived here some 3,500 years ago. Look out for them as you sail by. Zhu Xi, the Song dynasty Confucian scholar, lived on Wuyi Mountain for many years and founded the Ziyang Academy below Yinping Peak.

The wider Wuyi Reserve has a wide variety of flora and fauna and is a great place for hiking and birdwatching.

✚ 5J ✉ Northwest Fujian Province 🕐 Daily
6:30–6:30 💲 Expensive 🚃 Daily from Fuzhou,
Quanzhou, Xianmen ✈ Airport south of
Wuyishan City

YONGDING

The countryside in Yongding, Fujian Province, is dotted with circular fortress-type houses built 300 years ago by the Hakka, a Han ethnic minority, to protect themselves from attack. Many Hakka families still live in these circular dwellings, known locally as *tulou* (earth houses). They are simple but solid buildings made of packed earth. The largest is capable of housing up to 40 families. Each building comes with a hall, kitchen, storehouse, bedrooms and a well for water.

The Hakka have their own dialect and customs. Unlike other Han women, Hakka women never followed the custom of binding their feet.

The county was named Yongding, 'forever settled', at the end of Ming Dynasty, when Hakka refugees fled here to escape from war. About 20,000 *tulou* remain in the countryside, providing a startling sight when spotted from mountain roads above. Some of the finest examples of *tulou* architecture are at **Chengqilou,** Qiaofulou, Zhengfulou, and Huaijilou. The best way to view Hakka architecture is to hire a car and driver in the city of Yongding and head out to the countryside.

✚ 4K ✉ Southwest Fujian Province

🚌 Regular buses from Guangzhou, Xiamen. Minibuses from Yongding to Chengqilou

Chengqilou

✉ A 30-min taxi ride north of Yongding

🕓 Daily 👋 Inexpensive

Guangxi Province

GUILIN

The beautiful limestone karst scenery of Guilin has been celebrated throughout history. There are notable peaks within the city, including the 152m-tall (500ft) Solitary Beauty Peak (Duxiu Feng) and Folded Brocade Hill (Diecai Shan) in the northeast of the city, as well as Seven Star Park (Qixing Gongyuan). However, the focal point of any visit must be the Li River boat ride between Yangshuo and Guilin where hundreds of sugarloaf-shaped mountains rear up from the riverbank.

Many of Guilin's karst peaks contain fabulous caves with magnificent stalagmites and stalactites. It's easy to reach them by bicycle. It is also possible to take a trip with a fisherman using cormorants to catch fish. The trained birds – which have a leash around their necks to keep them from swallowing their catch – dive for fish and then deposit their catch on the bamboo raft. The main ethnic group here is the Zhuang, the largest of China's 55 minority groups.

🚽 2K ✉ 590km (367 miles) northwest of Guangzhou, Guangxi Province 🚌 Buses from Yangshuo, Nanning 🚆 Guilin Train Station ✈ Guilin International Airport

Li River Cruise

✉ All cruises begin at the Zhujiang (Bamboo River) Pier, 20km (12.5 miles) southeast of Guilin ☎ (0773) 282 5502 🕐 Daily 8:40am, 9:20am, 10:10am ✋ Expensive (includes lunch and return by bus)

YANGSHUO

Best places to see, ➤ 54–55.

Guizhou Province

Guizhou, in southwest China, remains relatively untouched by commercial tourism. Home to the Miao and several other minorities, Guizhou offers beautiful landscapes, with limestone karst hills, terraced rice fields, and rustic minority villages. Use Guiyang as a point for visits to nearby villages. In Jichang you will see women dressed in Ming Dynasty costumes and many Ming-style houses.

✚ 1K ✉ Guizhou Province 🚌 Local buses to local minority villages
🚆 Daily from Beijing, Chengdu, Chongqing, Guangzhou, Kunming

ANSHUN

This pleasant city, set amid limestone karst hills, is a major jumping off point for two of Guizhou's most spectacular sights. Around 120km (75 miles) north of Anshun is the **Zhijin Cave.** At 10km (6 miles) in length, and with cathedral-like galleries that reach a height of 150m (492ft) in parts, Zhijin is one of the largest caves in the world. Southwest of Anshun are the **Huangguoshu Falls.** With a width of 81m (88yds) and a height of 74m (80yds), the main waterfall is one of most spectacular in China. Within the surrounding hills is a matrix of caves and underground streams. The best time to visit is between May and October.

✚ 1K
🚌 Buses to Guiyang 🚆 Services to Kunming, nearby Guiyang and Chongqing
Zhijin Cave
✉ 15km (9 miles) north of Zhijin Town ☎ (0857) 781 2063 🕐 8:30–5
🚌 Buses to Zhijin from Anshun. Minibuses to Zhijin Cave
Huangguoshu Falls
✉ 45km (28 miles) southwest of Anshun ☎ (0853) 359 2766 🕐 6:30am–7pm
🚌 Regular buses from Anshun ✋ Expensive

ZHAOXING

Zhaoxing is the largest of the many Dong villages that pepper the rice terraced hills of Guizhou's southeastern fringe. The village is divided into five sections, each belonging to a different Dong clan and each with its own wooden drum tower and Wind and Rain Bridge. These attractive bridges function as lively outdoor social clubs, capable of standing up to anything Guizhou's temperamental weather can throw at them – hence their name. Evening cultural performances feature choral singing and lusheng bamboo pipe music that seems as much about entertaining the locals as about pleasing tourists.

➕ 2K ✉ Guizhou Province 🚌 Express buses connect nearby Kaili with Guiyang and Sanjiang with Guilin. Minibuses make onward trip to Zhaoxing 🚆 Nearest station in Kaili ✈ Nearest airports in Guiyang and Guilin

Hainan Province

SANYA

Located on the southern tip of Hainan, Sanya has become a playground for China's emerging jet set. With white sand beaches, whispering palm trees and a slew of top hotels, Hainan is avidly marketed as the 'Hawaii of the Orient'. The glamour of the natural surrounds is topped up in November when 100-plus Miss World wannabes arrive to compete in the annual contest. Hainan may not have Hawaii's fearsome breakers, but the tranquil ocean is perfect for windsurfing, jet-skiing, snorkelling and scuba-diving. Hainan is home to three of China's 55 minority groups and examples of their distinct culture can be found in the highland villages. A word of caution: the commercialization of minority culture – a problem throughout China – is particularly acute around Sanya. For a more authentic experience, head inland.

✚ 5M (inset) ✉ Sanya City, Hainan Island
🚌 Regular services to Haikou
🚆 Nearest station is in Haikou, which has direct services to mainland China (crossing made by loading rail carriages onto a ferry)
✈ Sanya International Airport

Hunan Province

WULINGYUAN

Wulingyuan is nature's reflection of China's newfangled high-rise cities. Around 3,000 quartzite spires shoot up from a deep valley vault, each a gravity defying compression of slate. This stunning national park in northwest Hunan Province is one of China's most remarkable geological oddities. The expensive $248 ticket buys two days' entry to Wulingyuan, and free use of the bus network inside the park. Use your time to visit each of the park's three areas, Zhangjiajie Forest Park, Tianzi Mountain and the Suoxi Valley, each connected by trails. Stone staircases allow fitter visitors to climb to the peaks. There are two cable cars but the highlight has to be the Bailong Lift (Bailong Dianti). It is attached to a sheer rock face and whisks guests up 326m (1,070ft) in 118 seconds. According to the *Guiness Book of Records*, it's the tallest outdoor elevator in the world.

🚌 2H 🖂 Park entrance is 30km (18.5 miles) from Zhangjiajie City
☎ (0744) 571 2595 🚌 Minibuses from Zhangjiajie City
🚆 Zhangjiajie City has services to Changsha and Yichang 💵 Expensive

HOTELS

GUANGZHOU
Shamian Hotel ($)
Situated on the south of Guangzhou's delightful Shamian Island, this is a good value, safe and clean budget option.
✉ 52 Shamiannan Jie ☎ (020) 8121 8359/8288

White Swan Hotel (Baitian'e Binguan) ($$$)
With a perfect view of the Pearl River this is arguably the best hotel in town, despite it also being Guangzhou's oldest five-star. Superb facilities include two swimming pools, fitness centre, indoor and outdoor tennis courts and a number of fine restaurants.
✉ 1 Shamian Nanjie, Shamian Island ☎ (020) 8188 6968; www.whiteswanhotel.com

GUILIN
Hotel of Modern Art (HOMA) ($$)
Extraordinary pyramid-shaped hotel located within the grounds of Yuzi Paradise, China's first dedicated to modern art. The expansive estate is surrounded by limestone karst peaks and contain more than 200 sculptures by international artists.
✉ Dabu Town, Yanshan District, Guilin (halfway between Guilin and Yangshuo) ☎ (0773) 386 5555; www.yuzi-paradise.com

HONG KONG
Hong Kong Hostel ($)
HK Hostel may be cheap but in terms of location it's unparalleled. Located in a residential block bang in the middle of Causeway Bay, the HK Hostel offers modest home comforts in clean rooms.
✉ 3rd Floor, Block A, 47 Paterson Street, Causeway Bay ☎ (852) 2392 6868; www.hostel.hk

Landmark Mandarin Oriental ($$$)
This chic hotel is connected to the fashionable Landmark shopping mall. Flatscreen TVs are built into the bathroom's crescent-shaped wall and a socket conects your iPod to the stereo system.
✉ 15 Queen's Road, Central ☎ (852) 2132 0188; www.mandarinoriental.com

Salisbury YMCA ($$)

Don't be fooled by the name. The YMCA has some of the most sought-after rooms in Hong Kong thanks to its superb location at the tip of the Kowloon Peninsula.

✉ 41 Salisbury Road, Kowloon ☎ (852) 2268 7888; www.ymcahk.org.hk

MACAU
Pousada de Sao Tiago ($$$)

Located at the tip of the Macau Peninsula with a superb view of the Pearl River Delta. The hotel is built into the site of a Portuguese fort.

✉ Avenida de Republica, Fortaleza de Sao Tiago da Barra ☎ (0853) 2837 8111; www.saotiago.com.mo

ZHANGJIAJIE
Xiangdian International Hotel ($$)

Rooms are based around peaceful courtyards and the glass-domed roof of the Restaurant has views of the mountain peaks.

✉ Zhangjiajie Forest Park, Zhangjiajie ☎ (0744) 571 2999; www.xiangdianhotel.com

RESTAURANTS

GUANGZHOU
Banxi Jiujia ($$)

Historic restaurant that remains popular for its dim sum delicacies and other Cantonese favourites.

✉ 151 Longjinxi Lu ☎ (020) 8181 5955 🕐 Breakfast, lunch and dinner

Black Swan Dumpling Restaurant ($)

Northern-style dumplings as well as meat dishes.

✉ 486 Huanshi Lu, 2nd floor ☎ (020) 8767 5687 🕐 Lunch, dinner

Guangzhou Restaurant ($$)

A local favourite, this old eatery specializes in seafood and the Cantonese dim sum.

✉ 2 Wenchangnan Lu ☎ (020) 8138 08083 🕐 Breakfast, lunch and dinner

Lotus Restaurant ($$)

Excellent dim sum restaurant serving Cantonese snacks and
noodles from pushcarts.

✉ 67 Dishipu Lu ☎ (020) 8181 3388 🕐 Breakfast, lunch and dinner

HONG KONG
Aqua Roma & Aqua Tokyo ($$$)

Located on the top floor of TST's tallest harbour-front tower, Aqua
Roma (Italian) has a floor-to-ceiling arched glass façade facing the
harbour while Aqua Tokyo (Japanese) looks out over Kowloon's
glittering urban cityscape. The Aqua Spirit cocktail bar is located
just above on the mezzanine floor.

✉ 29th Fl, 1 Peking Road, Tsim Sha Tsui, Hong Kong ☎ (852) 3427 2288;
www.aqua.com.hk 🕐 Lunch, dinner

Craftsteak ($$)

The best of the many international bistros along Elgin Street, one
of Central's most popular dining areas. The open plan kitchen
complements the Italian-café themed dining space. Set lunches
are good value here.

✉ 29 Elgin Street, Soho, Central ☎ (852) 2526 0999

The Felix ($$$)

Incredible location on the 28th floor of the Peninsula Hotel serving
a mix of European and Asian dishes.

✉ The Peninsula, Salisbury Road, Tsim Sha Tsui ☎ (852) 2315 3188;
www.hongkong.peninsula.com 🕐 Lunch, dinner

Tai Ping Koon ($)

Tai Ping Koon has been around since 1860 and is the pick of
Causeway Bay's famed 'soy sauce restaurants' that dress western
food up in a quintessentially Cantonese way.

✉ 6 Pak Sha Road, Causeway Bay ☎ (852) 2576 9161

The Verandah ($$$)

The restaurant of choice of Repulse Bay's moneyed residents
offers European fine dining in a seaside locale. The balcony area

has views across the lawns toward Hong Kong's best sand beach.
✉ South Wing, The Repulse Bay Hotel, 109 Repulse Bay Road, Repulse Bay
☎ (852) 2812 2722

MACAU
Clube Militar (The Military Club)
One of Macau's most atmospheric dining halls. This striking
colonial building was once a private club for military officers but
now serves up Portuguese fare.
✉ 975 Avenida da Praia Grande ☎ (853) 2871 4000

XIAMEN
Gulang Xinyu Restaurant (Gulangyu Island) ($$$)
Excellent fresh seafood dishes.
✉ 4 Zhonghua Lu ☎ (0592) 206 3073 🕐 Lunch, dinner

YANGSHUO
Café China ($$)
Boasting Yangshuo's only rooftop dining terrace, Café China
represents a romantic spot to sit and watch the sun set over the
nearby karst peaks.
✉ 34 West Street, Yangshuo ☎ (0773) 882 7744 🕐 Lunch, dinner

Le Votre ($$)
Located in an attractive wooden dining hall, Le Votre specializes in
French food but runs a nice sideline in deep fried snake, among
other tasty local treats. There's an outdoor dining area for the
warmer summer months.
✉ 79 West Street, Yangshuo ☎ (0773) 882 8040 🕐 Lunch, dinner

SHOPPING
ARTS AND CRAFTS
Amazing Grace Elephant Company
A multitude of arts and crafts from all over East Asia. A great place
to find unusual gifts.
✉ Star House, 5C1, Ground Floor, Harbour City, Kowloon, Hong Kong
☎ (852) 2730 5455

Eastern Dreams

Reproduction furniture, screens, ceramics and woodcarvings.

✉ 47A Hollywood Road, Central, Hong Kong ☎ (852) 2544 2804

BOOKS

Page One

Huge English-language bookshop, the best in Hong Kong.

✉ Times Square, 1 Matheson Street, Causeway Bay, Hong Kong
☎ (852) 2506 0383

DEPARTMENT STORES

Festival Walk

Festival Walk has the largest book shop and cinema in town and a huge ice rink too.

✉ 80–88 Tat Chee Avenue, Kowloon, Hong Kong ☎ (852) 2844 2222;
www.festivalwalk.com.hk 🕙 10–midnight

Harbour City

This goliath shopping complex comprises most of the western fringe of the Kowloon Peninsula and has four well-packed storeys.

✉ 3–9 Canton Road, Kowloon, Hong Kong ☎ (852) 2118 8666;
www.harbourcity.com.hk 🕙 10–9

IFC Mall

Strung between the two huge International Finance Center (IFC) towers, this new mall is open, spacious and contains just about every major chain store.

✉ 8 Finance Street, Central, Hong Kong ☎ (852) 2295 3308;
www.ifc.com.hk 🕙 10:30–10

The Landmark

Hong Kong's most fashionable mall now houses nothing but five-star brands, and includes items from all the big names in luxury retail. It also has the first Asian branch of London department store Harvey Nichols.

✉ 12–16 Des Voeux Road, Central, Hong Kong ☎ (852) 2525 4142;
www.centralhk.com 🕙 10:30–7:30

Langham Place

With around 300 stores spread over 15 storeys, this building is at the heart of an attempt to rejuvenate down-at-heel Mongkok.

✉ 8 Argyle Street, Mongkok, Hong Kong ☎ (852) 3520 2800; www.langhamplace.com.hk 🕐 10:30–11

Pacific Place

One of the most democratic of Hong Kong Island's malls, Pacific Place has a variety of indie stores.

✉ 88 Queensway, Admiralty, Hong Kong ☎ (852) 2844 8988; www.pacificplace.co.hk 🕐 10:30–11

Times Square

Times Square's twin towers rise to 46 and 39 storeys, the bottom 16 of which house a combination of international chains and local dealers, plus four storeys of restaurants and a cinema complex.

✉ 1 Matheson Street, Causeway Bay, Hong Kong ☎ (852) 2118 8900; www.timessquare.com.hk 🕐 10–10

ENTERTAINMENT

ARTS

Hong Kong Arts Centre

This is the strange-shaped building that juts out into Victoria Harbour. It has a busy schedule for film and the performing arts.

✉ 2 Harbour Road, Wanchai, Hong Kong ☎ (852) 2582 0200; www.hkac.org.hk

Hong Kong Cultural Centre

The Cultural Centre is the home of the Hong Kong Philharmonic Orchestra – one of the best orchestras in the world.

✉ 10 Salisbury Road, Tsim Sha Tsui, Hong Kong ☎ (852) 2734 9011; www.lcsd.gov.hk/hkcc

Hong Kong Fringe Club

Plays host to a variety of alternative performers – jazz, theatre, poetry, classical music, and Hong Kong's annual City Festival.

✉ 2 Lower Albert Road, Central, Hong Kong ☎ (852) 2521 7251

COOKING
Yangshuo Cooking School
Half-day lessons in a village farmhouse begin with students shopping in a local market and then being taught to cook five specific dishes. You get to keep the recipes.

✉ Chaolong Village, Yangshuo, Guangxi province ☎ (137) 8843 7286
🕓 9:30am (also 3:30pm start, Mar–Nov) ✋ Expensive

OUTDOOR SHOWS
Symphony of Lights
Twenty of Hong Kong Island's tallest buildings become a canvas to a series of synchronised searchlights and lasers in this nightly display. The show begins at 8pm and last around 20 minutes. The Tsim Sha Tsui Promenade at the southern tip of Kowloon offers uninterrupted views.

Impression Liu Sanjie
A cast of 600 perform elegant routines on a floating set at the confluence of the Li and Yulong rivers. The backdrop is 12 karst limestone peaks, lit dramatically by spotlights.

✉ Li River Mountain-Water Theatre, Yangshuo ☎ (0773) 881 1982; www.yxlsj.com 🕓 Daily 7:40–8:50pm ✋ Expensive (from 188RMB)

SPORT
Hong Kong Horse Racing
Race meetings are held at Shatin in the New Territories most weekends during the season. The claustrophobic course at Happy Valley on Hong Kong Island has meetings most Wednesdays.

☎ www.hkjc.com 🕓 Sep–Jun ✋ Inexpensive

ADVENTURE
Macau Tower
This tower, 338m (1,110ft) tall, has a variety of thrilling rides and activities. The Mast Climb, Bungee Jump, SkyJump and Skywalk X all require a strong stomach.

✉ Largo da Torre de Macau ☎ (853) 2893 3339; www.macautower.com.mo
🕓 Mon–Fri 10–9, Sat–Sun 9–9 ✋ Moderate–expensive

Western China

The western half of China is a remarkably diverse region, stretching from the steamy jungles of Yunnan, close to the Burmese border, all the way to the deserts of Xinjiang, via the snow-capped peaks of Tibet and Sichuan. Compared to the densely populated eastern half of the country, the west is wild and desolate, with little industry.

Chengdu
□

The culture is as varied as the topography. A rich Buddhist and Muslim heritage can be found in Gansu and Xinjiang provinces, where you can visit oasis cities along the ancient Silk Road, a route once travelled by camel caravans carrying goods between China and the mysterious western world. Known as the 'Roof of the World', Tibet is located on the vast, windswept Qinghai-Tibet Plateau, and is an average 4,060m (13, 321ft) above sea level. The huge Buddhist monasteries here are really something special too and worth making time to go and visit.

CHONGQING

Chongqing has a history going back more than 2,000 years. It was the capital of the ancient state of Ba in the Zhou Dynasty. The city was named an open treaty port in 1890, but attracted little foreign interest. Hongyan Cun, or **Red Crag Village,** served as the offices and residences for the Communist representatives during the alliance with the Nationalists during the war against the Japanese and a museum now stands on the site. These days Chongqing is one of the best places to observe the contrasts of modern China. As the economic powerhouse of the southwest, the city absorbs millions of migrants who spend their nights in the ghoulish grey tenement blocks and their days building towering skyscrapers. The city centre has been built into the steep hillsides around two huge waterways – the Yangtze and the Jialing. Two cableways connect

the riverbanks and offer great views of the downtown high-rises. With Chongqing's famously bad weather, it's a trip best made at night. Also in the city, is the US-Chiang Kaishek **Criminal Acts Exhibition Hall and SACO Prison,** which commemorate the jail set up by the Nationalists. The grim prison held hundreds of political prisoners under very harsh conditions. Chongqing is known as one of China's four 'furnaces' due to the stifling heat in summer. Avoid travel during this time if possible.

✚ 1H ✉ Chongqing Municipality, 300km (186 miles) southeast of Chengdu 🚌 Express buses to Chengdu, Dazu, Leshan 🚆 Daily from Chengdu, Beijing, Dazu, Kunming, Shanghai ✈ Jiangbei International Airport

Red Crag Village
✉ Hongyan Lu
☎ (023) 6330 0192
🕐 Daily 8.30–5
✋ Inexpensive
🚌 104 on Beiqu Lu

Exhibition Hall and SACO Prison
✉ Zhuangzhi Lu ☎ (023) 6531 3028 🕐 Daily 8–7 ✋ Inexpensive 🚌 217 on Zhongshan Lu

DAZU
The Dazu Buddhist Caves, 160km (100 miles) northwest of Chongqing, Sichuan Province, are divided among 40 different locations, and include more than 50,000 carvings from the Tang and Song dynasties. This is one of the most important Buddhist archaeological sites in China, predating other such sites by hundreds of years. The two most popular caves are Beishan and Baodingshan, each of which has around 10,000 sculptures.

The sculptures in **Baodingshan,** 15km (9 miles) northeast of Dazu, are said to be the most beautiful. They were made during the Southern Song Dynasty, and are scattered around 13 different sites. The sculptures were paid for with funds raised by Zhao Zhifeng, a monk who turned Baodingshan into a centre of Tantric Buddhism. Cave 8 is home to the largest 1,000-armed Buddha in China, which has an eye in each of its palms. The Great Buddha Crescent is the site of the most famous Buddha at Dazu, the Reclining Buddha entering Nirvana, which stretches 31m (102ft) from head to knees.

Beishan, just 2km (1.25 miles) north of Dazu, has 290 caves. The sculptures here were produced in the Tang Dynasty. This was a former military stronghold held by Wei Junjing, a Sichuan military leader who ordered the construction of the first Buddhist temple at Beishan. Cave 136, the best preserved and largest of the caves, shows Puxian, the patron deity of Mount Emei, riding a white elephant, and Guanyin, the Goddess of Mercy. It also has a large carved wheel representing the cycle of life and death. A pagoda sits on the top of the mountain.

✚ 14R ✉ 160km (100 miles) northwest of Chongqing, Chongqing Municipality 🍴 Street foodstalls on Shizi Jie 🚌 Daily to Chengdu, Chongqing

Baodinsan
✉ Baoding Zhen 🕐 Daily 8–5 ✋ Moderate 🚌 Take a long-distance bus from Chongqing

Beishan
✉ Baoding Zhen, Beishan 🕐 Daily 8–5 ✋ Moderate 🚌 Take a long-distance bus from Chongqing

Gansu and Qinghai Provinces

Gansu is a large but sparsely populated desert province that runs diagonally between the Mongolian steppe and the Qinghai-Tibetan Plateau.

MOGAO KU (MOGAO CAVES)

Best places to see, ➤ 50–51.

QINGHAI HU (QINGHAI LAKE)

Qinghai Lake is a salt water lake in northeast Qinghai Province, 300km (186 miles) from Xining. It is the largest inland lake in China, covering an area of 4,455sq km (1,720sq miles) and with a circumference of 900km (560 miles). Called the Western Sea in ancient times, the lake was formed around a million years ago. Qinghai Lake is surrounded by mountains, and more than 50 rivers run into it. It's drained by the Yellow River and its tributaries. Bird Island, located on the western side of the lake, is the largest breeding ground for birds in China, with some 12 species migrating here from India and southern China to breed from March to early June. Birds found here include wild geese, gulls, cormorants, sandpipers, and the rare black-necked cranes.

✚ 12Q ✉ 155km (96 miles) from Xining, Qinghai Province 🚌 Regular buses from Xining to Heimahe ❓ Tours to Bird Island can be booked in Xining

Sichuan Province

Sichuan is of China's oldest and most populated provinces. Much of it lies in the fertile Sichuan Basin making it an important agricultural area. However, the western and northern reaches of the province are characterized by snowy mountain peaks and wild landscapes, making it one of China's most beautiful areas.

CHANG JIANG (YANGTZE RIVER)

Best places to see, ➤ 40–41.

CHENGDU

The capital of Sichuan Province is one of China's fastest growing cities, combining modern, tree-lined avenues with older areas of

traditional, half-timbered houses. One such traditional house is **Du Fu's Thatched Cottage.** Du Fu (712–770), one of China's greatest poets, retired here in 759, writing 240 poems during his three-year stay. In the Song Dynasty, a thatched cottage was erected on the site of the original cottage, and was later expanded to include a garden, making it a pleasant place for a stroll.

The **Wenshu Yuan** temple was founded in the 6th century and is the headquarters of Zen (Chan) Buddhism in China. The temple, which is dedicated to the God of Wisdom, was destroyed in fighting during the Ming Dynasty, and rebuilt in 1691. The bustling street in front of the temple is also worth visiting, with peddlers selling incense, candles, prayer beads and ghost money. Also worth visiting is **Wuhouci** (Wuhou Temple), a series of memorial halls dedicated to Zhu Geliang, a military hero from Chinese lore. The temple was founded in the fifth century, but was rebuilt in 1672, and was recently restored.

Sichuan is the home of China's lovable Giant Panda and around 10km (6 miles) north of Chengdu is the **Giant Panda Breeding Base**. The centre's breeding success means you'll likely be able to view new born clubs with their mothers, especially in the autumn.

✚ 13R ✉ Capital of Sichuan Province 🚌 Express buses to Chongqing, Leshan 🚆 Daily from Chongqing, Beijing, Guangzhou, Kunming, Shanghai, Xi'an ✈ Shangliu Airport

Du Fu's Thatched Cottage

✉ 38 Qinghai Lu ☎ www.dfmuseum.org.cn

🕐 Apr–Sep 7:30–7, Oct–Mar 8–6:30 🚌 301

Wenshu Yuan (Manjusiri Temple)

✉ 3 Duan Renmin Zhonglu 🕐 Daily 8–6 ✋ Inexpensive 🚌 55, 64

Wuhouci (Wuhou Temple)

✉ 231 Wuhouci Dajie ☎ (028) 8555 9027 🕐 Daily 8–6

🚌 1, 57, 59, 334

Giant Panda Breeding Base

✉ 26 Xiongmao Dadao, Futoushan ☎ (028) 8351 6748; www.panda.org.cn

🕐 Daily 7–6 ✋ Moderate

EMEISHAN (MT EMEI)

One of China's four sacred Buddhist Mountains, Emeishan represents Puxian, the Bodhisattva of Universal Kindness, usually seen riding a white elephant. Emeishan is covered with bamboo, fir trees, pine trees and a variety of plants and flowers, and has a wide variety of butterflies, birds, monkeys, and even pandas on its more remote slopes. There are two trails up the mountain, which at 3,000m (9,483ft), is a tough climb. The northern route is shorter and more direct. There are about 30 temples on the mountain, the most famous of which is Baoguo Temple, considered the gateway to Emeishan. The walk up and down the mountain can take two to four days, but there are hostels along the way to break up the trip. For those seeking an easier route there are buses running to a point half way up, where you can transfer to a cable car after a short walk.

🕇 13R ✉ 6.5km (4 miles) west of Emei Town, 35km (22 miles) west of Leshan, Sichuan Province

☎ (0833) 559 0111; www.ems517.com 🕒 24 hours

🚌 Regular buses between Leshan and Emei Town

🚆 Daily from Chengdu, Kunming 🖐 Expensive

JIUZHAIGOU NATIONAL PARK

Tucked away in the mountains of northern Sichuan, Jiuzhaigou is a series of three interconnected valleys which have colourful forest canopies, gushing waterfalls and aquamarine lakes, all framed against a snowy mountain backdrop. The Chinese name translates as 'nine village valley', referring to the original Tibetan settlements that dotted the landscape. Though there are still a few prayer wheels

and Tibetan stupa, the three remaining villages have lost much of their appeal and can hardly be described as attractions in their own right. The main motivation for modern visitors is the spectacular alpine scenery. It's more than 30km (18.5 miles) from the entrance, in the north, to the most southerly extremity of the park which lies 3,060m (10,040ft) above sea-level. Shuttle buses whisk travellers around and set off every ten minutes.

➕ 13R ✉ Jiuzhaigou County, 435km north of Chengdu
☎ (0837) 773 9753; www.jiuzhaigouvalley.com/english
🕐 1 Apr–15 Nov 7–7:30; 16 Nov–31 Mar 8– 5:30
🚌 Daily departures for Chengdu 🖐 Expensive
✈ Jiuzhaigou Huanglong Airport, Daily flights to Chengdu

LESHAN

Carved in the face of a cliff in the Tang Dynasty, Leshan's Maitreya Buddha gazes calmly over the confluence of the Min, Dadu and Qingyi rivers.

The statue is the largest carved stone Buddha in the world. It is known in Chinese simply as Dafo, or the Big Buddha. The seated statue is 71m (232ft) tall. The head alone is 14.7m (48ft), the ears 7m (23ft) long. The statue can be viewed by boat from the river, or by climbing to the top of the hill next to where the statue stands and then descending the steps to its foot.

➕ 13R ✉ 115km (71 miles) south of Chengdu, Sichuan Province ☎ (0833) 230 2416; www.leshandafo.com
🕐 Apr–7 Oct daily 7:30–7:30; 8 Oct–Mar daily 8–6
🚌 Regular buses to Chengdu. From Leshan city, take bus 3 or 13 to the park gate 🖐 Moderate 🚢 Tour boats leave Leshan pier every 30 mins, daily 7–5

Tibet Autonomous Region

Tibetan culture prospered during the 10th to the16th centuries. In the 18th century China made Tibet a protectorate, and began to control the Dalai Lamas. Tibet became relatively independent after the 1911 revolution, but was seized by China in 1951 by soldiers of the People's Liberation Army.

GANDEN GOMPA (GANDEN MONASTERY)

Ganden Monastery, built in the early 15th century by Tsongkhapa, is today home to several hundred Buddhist monks. The monastery was seriously damaged during the Cultural Revolution. A stupa at the monastery holds the remains of Tsongkhapa, founder of the Yellow Hat Sect of Tibbetan Buddhism.

✚ 10R ✉ 45km (28 miles) east of Lhasa 🕔 Daily 9–4 ✋ Moderate

GYANTSE

Travellers to Shigatse often stop off at Gyantse, situated at the juncture of two important caravan routes to India and Nepal. The city, Tibet's fourth largest, was important strategically, and was once a major trading centre for nomads. The **Palkhor Monastery,** built in the 1427, has been badly damaged, but is worth visiting, especially its Nepalese Kumbun stupa with painted eyes and beautiful murals. The city's old fort, or Dzong, which overlooks the city, was hit by British artillery in 1904 and again by the People's Liberation Army in 1960.

✠ 10R ⊠ 255km (158 miles) southwest of Lhasa, Tibet

🚌 Minibuses from Lhasa via Shigatse

Palkhor Monastery

⊠ Gyantse ⏰ Daily 10–7 ✋ Moderate

LHASA

Best places to see, ➤ 46–47.

SAMYE

Samye Monastery, the first Buddhist monastery to be built in Tibet, was founded by an Indian scholar, the abbot Shantarakshita, during the reign of King Trisong Detsen in the 8th century.

✠ 10R ⊠ Approximately 30km (19 miles) west of Tsetang ⏰ Daily 8–6 ✋ Inexpensive

SHIGATSE

Located in the valley of the Yarlong Tsangpo River (known in India as the Brahmaputra), Shigatse is the second largest urban area in Tibet. The city was dominated by the Red Hat Sect until the arrival of the fifth Dalai Lama, who defeated the sect with the support of the Mongolians, uniting the country under the Yellow Hat Sect. The beautiful Tashilhunpo Monastery, the seat of the Panchen Lama, was built here in 1447. The terraced monastery has a 28m (92ft) statue of the Maitreya Buddha and a Grand Hall that houses the tomb of the fourth Panchen Lama.

✠ 9R ⊠ 250km (155 miles) southwest of Lhasa 🚌 Minibuses from Lhasa

Yunnan Province

DALI

The old walled town of Dali sits on the edge of Erhai Lake, with the Azure (Cangshan) Mountains a beautiful backdrop. The main ethnic group is the Bai, believed to have built settlements here 3,000 years ago, and known for their colourful dress and embroidery. The Bai defeated Tang troops in the 8th century to establish the Nanzhao Kingdom which, at its height, spread to parts of Burma and Laos. Nanzhao, later renamed Dali, remained independent until 1253, when it was conquered by the Mongols led by Kublai Khan, who made it part of his empire.

The main street, Huguo Lu, is lined with restaurants and shops selling embroidery, batiks, and marble. **The Three Pagodas,** northwest of the city, were built during the Tang Dynasty. The restored Chongsheng Temple, behind the three pagodas, is a

good example of the traditional temple architecture of
Yunnan Province.

➕ 12T ✉ 300km (186 miles) west of Kunming, Yunnan
Province 🍴 Restaurants along Boai Lu and Huguo Lu
🚌 Buses from Xiaguan, Lijiang and Kunming
✈ Xiaguan Airport (45 minutes from Dali)

The Three Pagodas
✉ 2km (1 mile) northwest of Dali 🕐 Daily 7–7 ✋ Moderate

LIJIANG
Best places to see,
➤ 48–49.

XISHUANGBANNA
Located in a subtropical
region in southwest
Yunnan Province,
Xishuangbanna borders

Burma and Laos. According to the indigenous Dai
people, Xishuangbanna was discovered thousands of
years ago by hunters chasing golden deer. When the
Mongols invaded China in the 13th century, the Dai
fled south to this area, which was soon made part of
the Chinese empire. Despite this, they managed to
retain their own language and customs. Jinghong, the
capital of the Xishuangbanna Dai Autonomous
Prefecture, is a jumping off point for trips to
surrounding stilt villages. The most important annual
event is the Water Splashing Festival in mid-April, a
celebration of Dai New Year.

➕ 12T ✉ Southern Yunnan Province 🚌 Buses to Kunming
✈ Jinghong International Airport (5km/3 miles south of town).
Daily flights to Kunming
❓ Water Splashing Festival, 13–15 Apr

Xinjiang Autonomous Region

The Xinjiang Uighur Autonomous Region is the largest province in China. The population is primarily made up of Arabic, Turkic-speaking peoples of Central Asian extraction.

KASHGAR

Kashgar, located in the Xinjiang Autonomous Region near the border with Pakistan, is the westernmost town in China. The city, which opened to visitors in 1985, remains primarily Central Asian, with little Chinese flavour. In ancient times, Kashgar was one of the most important oasis towns on the Silk Road between the Middle East and China. The 1986 opening of the Karakorum Highway, linking China and Pakistan, bolstered the city's position as an important transport hub.

Some 150,000 people visit the Sunday Market, just 2km (1.25 miles) from the centre of town, each Sunday to purchase metal ware, jewellery, rugs, pottery, musical instruments and spices as well as to sample traditional Central Asian specialities, such as naan bread and mutton kebabs. Centrally located, the **Id Kah Mosque** is one of the largest mosques in China. It is believed to have been built in 1738 but has been renovated several times since. The mosque's main hall can accommodate about 20,000 worshippers.

In an eastern suburb of Kashgar stands the imposing **Mausoleum of Abakh Khoja** – a Muslim holy man – and five generations of his family. This domed structure is also said to be the burial place of Xiangfei, a beautiful concubine of the Qing Emperor Qianlong, believed to be Abakh Khoja's daughter.

✠ 7N ✉ Xinjiang Province, about 1,500km (932 miles) west of Urumqi
🍴 Uighur foodstalls outside the Id Kah Mosque 🚌 Buses to Kyrgyzstan, Pakistan and Urumqi 🚆 Daily from Urumqi ✈ Kashgar Airport (12km/7.5 miles northeast of town, but very few flights)

Id Kah Mosque
✉ Jiefang Beilu, west of Id Kah Square ☎ (0998) 282 7113 🕐 Daily 9–7
👤 Inexpensive

Mausoleum of Abakh Hoja
✉ Aizilaiti Lu ☎ (0998) 265 0630 🕐 Daily 10–dusk 👤 Inexpensive

TURPAN (TURFAN OR TULUFAN)

Once a major oasis town on the Silk Road between China and the Middle East, Turpan was also an important Buddhist centre, until migrations of Uighurs brought the area under the influence of Islam in the 8th century. Turpan is today an agricultural centre famous for sweet Hami melons, dates and grapes. The city is also known as the Land of Fire, due to its intense summer heat, which can top 40°C. Many famous 20th-century Western explorers and archaeologists came here to explore the nearby caves and shipped crates of sculptures, frescoes and other treasures and artefacts to Europe. The city has a busy Sunday bazaar, where colourful silk dresses and hats are a speciality. The circular Emin Minaret, at the Suleiman Mosque, was built in 1777 using unglazed mud bricks.

Bezeklik, located in the mountains outside the city, is a Buddhist cave with deteriorated carvings made between the 5th and 14th centuries. The ancient desert ruins of Jiaohe and Gaochang are a short drive out of town. Also nearby are the Flaming Mountains, so named because of their deep red hue.

➕ 10N ✉ 165km (103 miles) east of Urumqi, Xinjiang Province 🚌 Buses to Urumqi, minibuses to Daheyan 🚆 Daheyan Station 58km (36 miles) north of Turpan

Bezeklik

✉ Northwest of the Flaming Mountains 🕐 Daily 9–5 ✋ Moderate

HOTELS

CHENGDU

Crowne Plaza Chengdu ($$$)

The top hotel in Chengdu and situated in the heart of the city. Great restaurants and fitness facilities, and the popular Rainbow Crowne Nite Club is busy most nights.

✉ 31 Zhongfu Lu ☎ (028) 8678 6666; www.ichotelsgroup.com

Wen Jun Lou Hotel ($)

This pretty YHA-affliliated hotel takes shape in the style of Qing Mansion and has rooms set around two courtyards. A popular choice with younger travellers and a fairly social venue.

✉ 12 Qintai Lu, Chengdu ☎ (028) 8613 8884; www.dreams-travel.com/wenjun

CHONGQING

Hilton Chongqing ($$)

The Hilton Chongqing offers a slice of Shanghai class in the midst of the Chinese hinterland, with spacious rooms (some with views of the river) and a range of top-notch restaurants.

✉ 139 Zhongshan Sanlu ☎ (023) 8903 8558; www.hilton.com

Wudu Binguan ($$)

A standard, moderately priced hotel with a good French restaurant.

✉ 24 Shang Zhengjiayan, Zhongshansi Lu, Yuzhongqu ☎ (023) 6385 1788

DALI

Jim's Guesthouse (Heping Kezhan) ($)

Basic, comfortable rooms with 24-hour hot water. Still very popular with independent travellers.

✉ 63 Boai Lu, Dali Old Town ☎ (0872) 267 1822

Jinhua Hotel ($)

Located at the very heart of ancient Dali. All rooms provide cable television and the hotel has a friendly bar and lounge.

✉ Corner of Huguo Lu and Fuxing Jie ☎ (0872) 267 3343; www.dljhhotel.com

DAZU
Dazu Hotel ($)
Best location for visiting Beishan and Baodingshan. Amenities include a fitness centre and an in-house nightclub.

✉ 47 Gongnong, Longgang Town ☎ (023) 4372 2250

DUNHUANG
Silk Road Dunhuang Hotel (Dunhuang Shanzhuang) ($$)
Incredible location in the sand dunes south of town. The hotel provides every possible convenience including camel riding, sand sledding and archery.

✉ Dunyue Lu ☎ (0937) 888 2088; www.the-silk-road.com

EMEISHAN
Jinding Hotel ($$)
Situated just below the summit of 3,099m (10,168ft), the Jinding is an ideal place for a rest after climbing the sacred Buddhist mountain or bedding down before a sunrise visit to the peak.

✉ Golden Summit, Emeishan ☎ (0833) 509 8088

JIUZHAIGOU
Jiuzhai Paradise Holiday Resort ($$)
Nestled against the snow-capped mountains of north Sichuan. The highlight is the reception – a gigantic glass dome bubble with rock pools, rivers and bars set within recreated traditional buildings.

✉ Ganhaizi, Zhangzha Town, Jiuzhaigou County ☎ (0837) 778 9999; www.jiuzhaiparadise.com

KASHGAR
Qianhai Hotel ($)
A quiet, laid-back place with a few facilities including a restaurant.

✉ 199 Renminxi Lu ☎ (0998) 283 1805

LHASA
Lhasa Hotel ($$)
Comfortable three-star hotel with five restaurants and satellite television in every room. This place has hot water all year round,

something that cannot be said for some of Lhasa's other hotels.

✉ 1 Minzu Lu ☎ (0891) 683 2221

House of Shambhala ($$)

Hailed as the first boutique hotel in Tibet, this 10-room property is set in a restored Tibetan courtyard home.

✉ 7 Jiri Erxiang (just south of Barkhor Square) ☎ (010) 6402 7151; www.houseofshambhala.com

Kyichu Hotel ($$)

This friendly, family-run lodge is one of Lhasa's oldest private hotels and remains one of the classiest accommodation options in town.

✉ 149 Beijing Donglu, Lhasa ☎ (0891) 633 1541

TURPAN

Oasis Hotel (Luzhou Binguan) ($)

Facilities include an Internet café and sauna room. The restaurant serves excellent regional specialities.

✉ 41 Qingnianbei Lu ☎ (0995) 852 2491; www.the-silk-road.com/hotel/turpanoasishotel/index.html

RESTAURANTS

CHENGDU

Baguo Buyi Restaurant ($$)

One of Chengdu's more fashionable restaurants with branches across China. Specializes in traditionally spicy Sichuan fare. Ask after the 'clothes hanger' dish which features thin strips of cucumber and pork slices hanging over a wooden railing.

✉ 8 Guangfuqiao Beijie ☎ (028) 8551 1999 🕓 Lunch, dinner

Charley Johng's Café ($)

Serves decent Chinese and Western food and staff can help to buy tickets. Bike rental and internet also available.

✉ Mingshan Lu, opposite the stadium ☎ (0937) 883 3039 🕓 Breakfast, lunch and dinner

Chen Mapo Doufu Restaurant ($)

Prepares the spicy bean curd dish that made Chengdu famous as well as other Sichuan peppery favourites.

✉ 197 Xiyulong Jie ☎ (028) 8675 4512 🕐 Lunch, dinner

Dunhuang

If you're not put off by street stall food, try the bustling market to the south of Yangguan Dong Lu, nearly opposite the Dunhuang Museum, which serves a wide variety of inexpensive foods until around midnight.

Huangcheng Laoma Restaurant ($$)

Traditional Sichuan hotpot restaurant. Order meat and vegetables and cook them in the hotpot at your own table.

✉ 106 Qintai Lu ☎ (028) 8613 1752 🕐 Lunch, dinner

Long Chaoshou ($–$$)

Opened in 1940, this is one of Chengdu's oldest and most famous restaurants. The three floors serve different types of food.

✉ 48 South Chunxi Lu ☎ (028) 8666 6947 🕐 Breakfast, lunch, dinner

Shirley's Café ($)

Similiar to Charley Johng's (Shirley is said to be his sister).

✉ Mingshan Lu, opposite Charley Johng's Café ☎ (0937) 882 6387
🕐 Breakfast, lunch and dinner

DALI
Kai's Kitchen ($)

Good Tibetan and Western favourites, including fresh Yunnan coffee and desserts, served at a roadside café.

✉ 81 Huguo Lu ☎ (0872) 267 0598 🕐 Breakfast, lunch and dinner

Sunshine Café ($)

Simple Western, Bai and Chinese fare served by friendly staff in a laid-back setting. Hearty breakfasts served with some excellent Yunnan coffee.

✉ 16 Huguo Lu ☎ (0872) 266 0712 🕐 Lunch, dinner

EMEISHAN
Teddy Bear Café ($)
Popular with backpackers, this simple restaurant serves both Western and Sichuan dishes and does a good cup of coffee.

✉ 42 Baoguo Lu, on the road leading to Baoguo Monastery ☎ (0833) 559 0135; www.teddybear.com.cn 🕐 Breakfast, lunch and dinner

KASHGAR
Caravan Café ($$)
This comfortable travel agency-cum-eatery provides weary travellers with some much needed home culinary comforts, with Western breakfasts, as well as great coffees and cake.

✉ 120 Seman Lu ☎ (0998) 298 1864; www.caravancafe.com

LHASA
Lhasa Kitchen ($)
The Lhasa Kitchen has a great second-floor location nearby Jokhang Temple. It's popular with both the local monks and tourists and offers Western, Nepali and Indian cuisine.

✉ 3 Minchi Khang Donglu ☎ (0891) 634 8855)

Norling Restaurant ($$)
The terrace and courtyard garden of the Kyichu Hotel are a good al fresco option. A wide variety of Tibetan, Nepali and Indian dishes.

✉ Kyichu Hotel, 18 Beijing Zhonglu ☎ (0891) 633 1541; www.kyichuhotel.com

Old Mandala Restaurant ($)
Yak variations include sizzling steak and curry. Also offers miscellaneous world cuisine including Italian and Japanese dishes and some tasty desserts.

✉ 31 South Barkhor ☎ (0891 632 9645)

Snowlands Restaurant ($)
Inexpensive Chinese, Tibetan, Indian and Western dishes in an unpretentious setting.

✉ 4 Zangyiyuan Lu ☎ (0891) 633 7323 🕐 Breakfast, lunch and dinner

Urumqi
Try any of the small Arabic restaurants on Xinhua Lu or explore the
night market on Changjiang Lu.

LIJIANG
Blue Papaya ($)
Tasty Italian, Chinese and vegetarian dishes.
✉ 50 Guan Men, Old Town ☎ (0888) 661 2114; www.thebluepapaya.com

Mama Fu's ($)
Enjoy Chinese and Western dishes alfresco beside the canal.
✉ 76 Xinyi Jie, Mishi Xiang ☎ (0888) 512 2285 🕐 Lunch, dinner

Sakura Café ($)
Good Bai, Korean, Japanese and Western dishes, including hearty
breakfasts. For dessert try the excellent brownies or banana or
chocolate pancakes.
✉ 123 Cuiwenduan, Xinhua Lu, Old Town ☎ (0888) 518 7619 🕐 Breakfast,
lunch and dinner

SHOPPING

CHENGDU
Shu Brocade Academy
Weavers use traditional wooden looms to make silk, one of
Sichuan's most celebrated products. Next door is an embroidery
shop and a factory which offers tours to tourists.
✉ 268 Huanhua Nanlu ☎ (028) 8738 3891; www.cdsilk.com 🕐 8:30–6

LIJIANG
Blue Papaya
Associated with the Blue Papaya Cultural Exchange Academy and
adjacent restaurant, this also store runs a line of Tibetian antiques
which are fun to browse and hunt out a bargain.
✉ 50 Guan Men, Old Town ☎ (0888) 661 2114; www.thebluepapaya.com

Bunong Bells
Sells engraved bronze bells, the like of which were used by

itinerant traders along the old Yunnan-Tibet tea trading trail to attract local villagers.

✉ Dashi Qiao, Old Town ☎ (0888) 512 6638 🕒 8:30am–1:30am

ENTERTAINMENT

ARTS
NAXI ORCHESTRA

Tradtional Naxi and Chinese music is played on classical instruments by a white wispy bearded cohort under the direction of local legend Xuan Ke.

✉ Naxi Music Academy, Dong Dajie, Lijiang, Yunnan Province ☎ (0888) 512 7971 🕒 Daily 8–10pm ✋ Expensive

Dynamic Yunnan

Yang Liping, one of China's most celebrated dancers, directs sumptuous this homage to Yunnan's amazing cultural diversity. Choral routines of amazing energy portray the indigenous traditions of the province's 26 minority groups. The spectacular may be expensive but it's worth every penny.

✉ Kunming Huitang Theatre, Kunming, Yunnan Province 🕒 Mon–Sat 8pm–9:30pm ✋ Expensive

MASSAGE
House of Shambhala Yoga-Spa Centre

Located within Lhasa's new boutique hotel, House of Shambhala hotel, this spa uses locally sourced products and oils.

✉ 7 Jiri Erxiang (just south of Barkhor Square), Lhasa, Tibet
☎ (010) 6402 7151 (Beijing office); www.houseofshambhala.com

SPORT

Shun Jiang Horse Trek Company

Offers guided treks up into the mountains that surround Songpan, close to Jiuzhaigou in northern Sichuan. A three day trek costs as little as 350RMB. It's well worth stopping in this beautiful mountain town for a night or two on the way to Jiuzhaigou.

✉ Songpan, Sichuan Province ☎ (0837) 723 1201

Index

Acknowledgements

The Automobile Association would like to thank the following photographers, companies and picture libraries for their assistance in the preparation of this book.

Abbreviations for the picture credits are as follows – (t) top; (b) bottom; (c) centre; (l) left; (r) right; (AA) AA World Travel Library.

4l Summer Palace AA/A Mockford & N Bonetti; **4c** Beijing airport AA/A Mockford & N Bonetti; **4r** Moon Hill, Yangshuo AA/D Henley; **5l** Erhai Lake, Dali AA/D Henley; **5c** Brushes AA/B Madison; **6/7** Summer Palace AA/A Mockford & N Bonetti; **8/9** Shanghai AA/A Mockford & N Bonetti; **10tr** Hall of Jade Ripples, Summer Palace AA/A Mockford & N Bonetti; **10cr** Temple of the Town Gods, Shanghai AA/G Clements; **10bl** Emperor's hat, AA/A Mockford & N Bonetti; **10/11** Temple of Heaven, Beijing AA/A Mockford & N Bonetti; **11tr** Yu Gardens, Shanghai AA/A Mockford & N Bonetti; **11br** Guilin AA/D Henley; **12tr** Food stall AA/G Clements; **12bl** Fortune cookie Photodisc; **12/13** Sanlitun Lu street, Beijing AA/A Mockford & N Bonetti; **13tl** TMSK Crystal Bar, Shanghai AA/A Mockford & N Bonetti; **13tr** Chopsticks Stockbyte Royalty Free; **13bl** Teashop, Houhai Lake, Beijing AA/A Mockford & N Bonetti; **14t** Pickles AA/G Clements; **14b** Beer AA/D Henley; **15** Chillis AA/B Madison; **16** Tiantan Park, Beijing; **16/17** Dried produce AA/D Henley; **17** Commuters AA/T Kaewdungdee; **18t** Tiananmen Square AA/A Mockford & N Bonetti; **18b** Peking duck AA/A Mockford & N Bonetti; **19** Tea house, Gu Shan island, Hangzhou; **20/21** Beijing airport AA/A Mockford & N Bonetti; **25** New Year, Yunnan AA/I Morejohn; **26** Shanghai airport AA/A Mockford & N Bonetti; **28/29** Xi'an AA/B Madison; **34/35** Moon Hill, Yangshuo AA/D Henley; **36** Terracotta warrior AA/B Madison; **36/37t** Terracotta warriors in rows AA/B Madison; **36/37b** Museum of Terracotta Warriors AA/B Madison; **38** Great Wall of China at Simatai AA/A Mockford & N Bonetti; **38/39** Great Wall of China at Simatai AA/G Clements; **39** Great Wall at Jiayuguan AA/I Morejohn; **40** Near Qutang Gorge AA/D Henley; **40/41** Ferry leaving Chongqing AA/A Kouprianoff; **42cr** Palace of Heavenly Purity AA/A Mockford & N Bonetti; **42b** Nine Dragons Screen AA/A Mockford & N Bonetti; **43** Cauldron AA/A Mockford & N Bonetti; **44** Lamma Island AA/B Bachman; **44/45t** View from The Peak AA/N Hicks; **44/45c** Man Mo Temple AA/N Hicks; **46** Man with prayer wheel AA/I Morejohn; **46/47** Potala Palace AA/I Morejohn; **48/49** Naxi musicians AA/I Morejohn; **49** Black Dragon Pond with Jade Dragon Snow Mountain beyond AA/D Henley; **50** Exterior of the caves AA/D Henley; **51** Mogao Caves AA/D Henley; **52** Tsingtao and Yanjing beer AA/A Mockford & N Bonetti; **52/53** Former German Governor's residence AA/I Morejohn; **54** Yangshuo AA/D Henley; **54/55** Karst peaks AA/D Henley; **56/57** Erhai lake, Dali AA/D Henley; **58** Place setting AA/A Mockford & N Bonetti; **60/61** Hutong AA/A Mockford & N Bonetti; **62** Huazang Temple, Emeishan AA/D Henley; **63** Camel train, Dunhuang AA/D Henley; **64/65** Hutong rooftops AA/A Mockford & N Bonetti; **65** Old hutong house AA/A Mockford & N Bonetti; **67** Light of Wisdom hall, Shanghai Science and Technology Museum AA/A Mockford & N Bonetti; **69** Great Wall at Simitai AA/G Clements; **70/71** Brushes AA/B Madison; **73** Tiananmen Square AA/A Mockford & N Bonetti; **74** Song Qing Ling AA/A Mockford & N Bonetti; **75** White Cloud Temple AA/A Kouprianoff; **76/77** Beihai Park AA/A Kouprianoff; **76c** Green dragon tiles AA/A Mockford & N Bonetti; **77b** Bronze astronomical instruments AA/G Clements; **78** Incense sticks AA/A Mockford & N Bonetti; **78/79b** Confucius Temple AA/G Clements; **79cr** Revolutionary statue AA/A Mockford & N Bonetti; **79br** Mao's Mausoleum AA/A Mockford & N Bonetti; **80** Qianmen AA/G Clements; **81** Changling AA/I Morejohn; **82t** Bedroom at Song Qing Ling Residence AA/A Mockford & N Bonetti; **82b** Gardens at Song Qing Ling Residence AA/A Mockford & N Bonetti; **83** Tiananmen Square AA/G Clements; **84tl** Hall of Prayer for Good Harvests AA/A Mockford & N Bonetti; Southern Cathedral interior AA/G Clements; **86/87** Garden of Harmonious Pleasure, Summer Palace AA/A Mockford & N Bonetti; **87tr** Bronze ox AA/A Mockford & N Bonetti; **88** Lama Temple AA/A Mockford & N Bonetti; **88/89** Ruins in the grounds of the Old Summer Palace AA/G Clements; **90tr** Gateway to Prince Gong's Mansion AA/A Mockford & N Bonetti; **90bl** Bar, Houhai Lake AA/A Mockford & N Bonetti; **91cl** Dog in basket AA/A Mockford & N Bonetti; **91br** Statue, Prince Gong's Mansion AA/A Mockford & N Bonetti; **92b** Puning Temple AA/D Henley; **92/93t** Locks placed by devotees AA/D Henley; **94t** Russian Matrioshka dolls AA/B Madison; **94/95c** St Sofia's Church AA/B Madison; **95** Drum Tower exterior, Xi'an AA/B Madison; **97** Drum Tower detail, Xi'an AA/B Madison; **98** Hanging Temple AA/I Morejohn; **98/99t** Woman harvesting grain AA/I Morejohn; **109** Humble Administrator's Garden, Suzhou AA/A Mockford & N Bonetti; **110/111** Pudong skyline AA/A Mockford & N Bonetti; **112t** French Concession AA/A Mockford & N Bonetti; **112/113** Fuxing Park, French Concession AA/A Mockford & N Bonetti; **113** Nanjing Road AA/G Clements; **114** The Bund AA/A Mockford & N Bonetti; **115** Tai chi AA/G Clements; **116** Oriental Pearl TV Tower AA/A Mockford & N Bonetti; **117** Chinese Ethnic Minorities Arts and Crafts Gallery, Shanghai Museum AA/A Mockford & N Bonetti; **118tl** Bust of Soong Qingling AA/G Clements; **118br** Sun Yatsen's Residence AA/G Clements; **118/119** St Ignatius Cathedral AA/G Clements; **120** Yu Garden AA/G Clements; **121** Woman in Jade Buddha Temple AA/A Kouprianoff; **122** Longmen Caves, near Luoyang AA/I Morejohn; **122/123t** Huangshan AA/I Morejohn; **122/123b** The Pagoda Forest, Shaolin Temple AA/I Morejohn; **124** Monk AA/D Henley; **124/125** Stone camel statues near Ming Xiaoling AA/A Mockford & N Bonetti; **125** Humble Administrator's Garden, Suzhou AA/A Mockford & N Bonetti; **126/127** Taishan AA/I Morejohn; **127b** Miniature statues of Confucius AA/T Kaewdungdee; **128** West Lake AA/D Henley; **129** Tea House lantern AA/D Henley; **139** View from The Peak, Hong Kong AA/D Henley; **140/141t** Waterfront Promenade, Kowloon AA/B Bachman; **140/141b** Causeway Bay and Wanchai Districts from Kowloon AA/B Bachman; **142tr** Po Lin Monastery AA/B Bachman; **142cl** Star ferry AA/B Bachman; **142/143** Peak Tram AA/B Bachman; **144/145** Bright Filial Piety Temple AA/D Henley; **146** Huaisheng mosque AA/D Henley; **146/147** Six Banyan Trees Temple AA/A Kouprianoff;

146bl Tai Chi AA/D Henley; **148/149** Gulangyu island AA/I Morejohn; **150/151** Rice paddies near Guilin AA/A Kouprianoff; **151br** Guilin AA/D Henley; **152** Bamboo AA/N Sumner; **152/153** Dong minority village © Iain Masterton/Alamy; **154** Sanya harbour AA/I Morejohn; **155** Limestone outcrops, Wulingyuan © Robert Harding Picture Library Ltd/Alamy; **163** Tashi-Lhunpo Monastery, Shigatse AA/I Morejohn; **164/165** Chongqing AA/D Henley; **165** Central Chongqing AA/D Henley; **166tr** Dazu AA/I Morejohn; **166/167** Qinghai Lake © Panorama Media (Beijing) Ltd/Alamy; **168/169** Du Fu's Thatched Cottage AA/D Henley; **170/171** Big Buddha, Leshan AA/D Henley; **172** Ganden monk AA/I Morejohn; **173** Palkhor Monastery, Gyantse AA/I Morejohn; **174** Bai wedding ceremony near Dali AA/D Henley; **174/175** The Three Pagodas AA/D Henley; **175** Rice paddies, Jinghong AA/I Morejohn; **176tl** Kashgar AA/D Henley; **176br** Sunday market AA/D Henley; **176/177** Hardware shop, Sunday market AA/D Henley; **178** Emin minaret, Suleiman mosque, Turpan AA/D Henley

Every effort has been made to trace the copyright holders, and we apologise in advance for any accidental errors. We would be happy to apply the corrections in the following edition of this publication.

Sight locator index

This index relates to the maps on the covers. We have given map references to the main sights of interest in the book. Grid references in italics indicate sights featured on town maps. Some sights within towns may not be plotted on the maps.

Dear Reader

Your comments, opinions and recommendations are very important to us. Please help us to improve our travel guides by taking a few minutes to complete this simple questionnaire.

You do not need a stamp (unless posted outside the UK). If you do not want to cut this page from your guide, then photocopy it or write your answers on a plain sheet of paper.

Send to: **The Editor, AA World Travel Guides, FREEPOST SCE 4598, Basingstoke RG21 4GY.**

Your recommendations...

We always encourage readers' recommendations for restaurants, nightlife or shopping – if your recommendation is used in the next edition of the guide, we will send you a **FREE AA Guide** of your choice from this series. Please state below the establishment name, location and your reasons for recommending it.

_____

_____

_____

_____

_____

Please send me **AA Guide** _____

About this guide...

Which title did you buy?

AA _____

Where did you buy it?_____

When? m m / y y

Why did you choose this guide? _____

_____

_____

_____

_____

Did this guide meet your expectations?

Exceeded ☐   Met all ☐   Met most ☐   Fell below ☐

Were there any aspects of this guide that you particularly liked? _____

_____

_____

_____

continued on next page...

Is there anything we could have done better? _____
_____
_____
_____

About you...
Name (Mr/Mrs/Ms) _____
Address _____
_____
_____ Postcode _____

Daytime tel nos _____
Email _____

Please only give us your mobile phone number or email if you wish to hear from us about
other products and services from the AA and partners by text or mms, or email.

Which age group are you in?
Under 25 ☐   25–34 ☐   35–44 ☐   45–54 ☐   55–64 ☐   65+ ☐

How many trips do you make a year?
Less than one ☐   One ☐   Two ☐   Three or more ☐

Are you an AA member? Yes ☐   No ☐

About your trip...
When did you book? m m / y y   When did you travel? m m / y y

How long did you stay? _____

Was it for business or leisure? _____

Did you buy any other travel guides for your trip? _____

If yes, which ones? _____
_____
_____

Thank you for taking the time to complete this questionnaire. Please send it to us as soon as
possible, and remember, you do not need a stamp (unless posted outside the UK).

AA Travel Insurance call 0800 072 4168 or visit www.theAA.com

---